Change by Design

Robert R. Blake
Jane Srygley Mouton
Anne Adams McCanse
Scientific Methods, Inc.

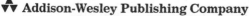 **Addison-Wesley Publishing Company**
Reading, Massachusetts • Menlo Park, California • New York
Don Mills, Ontario • Wokingham, England • Amsterdam • Bonn
Sydney • Singapore • Tokyo • Madrid • San Juan

Library of Congress Cataloging-in-Publication Data

Blake, Robert Rogers, 1918–

Change by design / by Robert R. Blake, Jane Srygley Mouton, Anne Adams McCanse.

p.   cm.

Includes bibliographical references.

ISBN 0-201-50748-X

1. Organizational change.   I.   Mouton, Jane Srygley.
II.   McCanse, Anne Adams.   III.   Title.
HD58.8.B55   1989
658.4'06—dc20

89-17621
CIP

This book is in the Addison-Wesley Series on Organization Development.
Editors: Edgar H. Schein, Richard Beckhard

ABCDEFGHIJ–BA–89

*Dr. Jane Mouton died unexpectedly on December 7, 1987.
Since this book represents her initiative in originating
Organization Development and the culmination of her
thirty-five year devotion to enriching the field, Change by Design
is dedicated to her memory.*

Other Titles in the Organization Development Series:

Developing Organizations: Diagnosis and Action
Paul R. Lawrence and Jay W. Lorsch

Organization Development:
Its Nature, Origins, and Prospects
Warren G. Bennis

Organization Development:
Strategies and Models
Richard Beckhard

Designing Complex Organizations
Jay Galbraith

Feedback and Organization Development:
Using Data-Based Methods
David A. Nadler

Matrix
Stanley M. Davis and Paul Lawrence

Career Dynamics:
Matching Individual and Organizational Needs
Edgar H. Schein

Organizational Dynamics:
Diagnosis and Intervention
John P. Kotter

Work Redesign
J. Richard Hackman and Greg R. Oldham

Pay and Organization Development
Edward E. Lawler

Managing Conflict:
Interpersonal Dialogue and Third-Party Roles
Second Edition
Richard E. Walton

Organization Development: A Normative View
W. Warner Burke

Foreword

The Addison-Wesley Series on Organization Development originated in the late 1960s when a number of us recognized that the rapidly growing field of "OD" was not well understood or well defined. We also recognized that there was no one OD philosophy, and hence one could not at that time write a textbook on the theory and practice of OD, but one could make clear what various practitioners were doing under that label. So the original six books by Beckhard, Bennis, Blake and Mouton, Lawrence and Lorsch, Schein, and Walton launched what has since become a continuing enterprise. The essence of this enterprise was to let different authors speak for themselves instead of trying to summarize under one umbrella what was obviously a rapidly growing and highly diverse field.

By 1981 the series included nineteen titles, having added books by Beckhard and Harris, Cohen and Gadon, Davis, Dyer, Galbraith, Hackman and Oldham, Heenan and Perlmutter, Kotter, Lawler, Nadler, Roeber, Schein, and Steele. This proliferation reflected what had happened to the field of OD. It was growing by leaps and bounds, and it was expanding into all kinds of organizational areas and technologies of intervention. By this time many textbooks existed as well that tried to capture the core concepts of the field, but we felt that diversity and innovation were still the more salient aspects of OD today.

The present series is an attempt both to recapture some basics and to honor the growing diversity. So we have begun a series of revisions of some of the original books and have added a set of new authors or old authors with new content. Our hope is to capture the spirit of inquiry and innovation that has always been the hallmark of organization development and to launch with these books a new wave of insights into the forever tricky problem of how to change and improve organizations.

We are grateful that Addison-Wesley has chosen to continue the series and are also grateful to the many reviewers who have helped us and the authors in the preparation of the current series of books.

Cambridge, Massachusetts   Edgar H. Schein
New York, New York   Richard Beckhard

Preface

We are now living through one of the most dramatic periods of change ever experienced by modern industrial society. Change is taking place daily everywhere, and the rate appears to be increasing rapidly. Its direction and tempo seem almost beyond our control. Can it be, in an age when we can transplant the human heart, put an astronaut in space, and decipher the genetic code that constitutes the very make-up of man, that we are powerless to control the institutions that we have so diligently created?

The deeper implications for remodeling corporate life require careful thought and attention. A strong, fundamental understanding of what is entailed in systemwide change as well as an ability to direct such an effort and to manage its rate offer the greatest possibility of achieving excellence throughout an entire organization. Being able to produce change and point it in the desired direction may indeed be one of our most profound intellectual assets. Mastering today's corporation and bringing it under the rein of human direction and control is the challenge we face, and the outcome may prove to be one of the truly great achievements of our age.

Change by Design deals with the fundamentals of planned change. The point of application is the corporation. This book describes the principles, concepts, and values behind Grid® Organization Development (Grid OD) and its methods of planned change. It presents the stages of development essential for inducing change and achieving desired results in an orderly, rigorous, and controlled way. The same principles with only slight modifications apply with equal impact to both profit-seeking and service-rendering organizations.

The strategies and tactics presented go beyond anything with which most people may have had direct experience. These strategies call for a different mind-set as they do not lie within the traditional realm of organization change. Therefore this book should be read as a departure from the more widely accepted rational strategies, quick fixes, and nostrums that have become so characteristic in today's management world. The point is to clear your thinking of traditional approaches to change and to take a fresh look at the possibilities offered by a systematic and integrated theory-based approach.

What follows can be read as a crystallization of our work in the field of organization development (OD) accompanied by extensive field notes collected through the years. Our observations of the state of the art of managing the use and development of human resources for productive outcomes are presented in many different illustrations and examples in order to clarify what may be required of managers in the unfolding commercial and service-oriented world of tomorrow.

The background for this approach was laid down some thirty years ago, at the origin of Grid OD. We see Grid OD as development that focuses on lifting the level of an entire organization to a higher plane of achievement. At the time of its conception, development rested on the presumption that if each individual considered independently was assisted to be more competent, the organization's level of competence could be expected to rise by virtue of strengthened individual capacities—this was known as the mosaic approach. Our belief lay in the premise that by focusing on individual, team, intergroup, and organization variables, rather than simply relying on the mosaic concept of individual development, a more realistic approach to change might be possible.

There is an element of truth implicit in the mosaic concept of individual development, yet it proves to be sorely lacking when viewed in terms of requirements of today's modern organization. When we begin to see that individuals do interact in teams rather than performing as independent units, and that individual development, as its name implies, focuses on the individual instead of team skills; when we recognize that groups must coexist in the presence of other groups where battles concerned with turf and territory often rule supreme; and when we realize with dismay that organization variables are not taken into consideration in providing overall leadership to the organization, then it becomes apparent that individual development is very much limited by virtue of the larger context within which individual competencies must be implemented.

To reiterate, most of today's approaches to human resource development are based on bits and pieces, each different from all the rest, sometimes appearing unique even when not directly made to appeal to some presumed consumer preference or other factor. Lost in such approaches unfortunately is the possibility of coherence, continuity, and comprehensiveness that are potentially available to help an organization become an integrated whole. The latter describes the path to the future. When an integrated approach such as Grid OD is relied on, organization members can acquire common values, shared goals, shared expectations, and a language for mutual communication and understanding.

If required to do so, based on our years of constant inquiry and efforts to induce change, the question might be posed, "Is there a big human resource problem that can be pointed to as having greater significance than any other?" Our answer is, "Yes, there is." This is the breakdown of mutual trust and confidence. There are probably a thousand influences that erode it, and many of these are illustrated in the chapters that follow. More important than what wears it down, however, is resolving the issue of how to restore it.

The answer to this lies in the second most important stumbling block in the area of human resources—the absence of openness and candor. When people are closed and hidden, there is little or no way to probe for intentions and, when intentions are misinterpreted, mutual trust and confidence fall to a low level. Openness and candor are the key for promoting mutual trust and confidence. That is, trust and confidence are central to cooperation, creativity, innovation, commitment, and synergistic achievements of many sorts. The good news is that openness and candor can be dealt with—it is an operational issue whether people are willing to do so, but we are all potentially capable of grasping the meaning of an open, forthright, self-revealing mind-set of mutuality.

A third barrier lying within the realm of human resources involves critique and feedback. It is a powerful tool that enables individuals to put it on the line, thereby bringing another person's attention to bear on an absence of readiness for open exchange, which is essential for candor as well as the development or restoration of mutual trust and confidence.

In summary, therefore, these three factors—mutual trust and confidence, openness and candor, and critique and feedback—can be thought of as the foremost barriers to effective utilization of human resources. Once an awareness is gained as to their effect on human interaction, they can be fully employed to maximize organization productivity.

Along these lines, we offer two suggestions for getting at the heart of this book, and that is to read it as a study of *organization* dynamics as opposed to a study of *individual* behavior. OD means development of the organization. To limit it to the scope of the individual is to miss the deeper implication of what is being presented, that is, how deeply the culture of a corporation controls the behavior of all its members. The ultimate objective of organization development is to liberate the people within it so that they can participate and contribute to problem solving. It is clear that corporate goals of profitability cannot be attained until the constraints that operate within the corporation's culture have been studied and deliberately rejected and removed. A key difference between individual and organization development is to be found in this proposition.

The second suggestion for reaching to the core of this book is that it is about *human values*. These are the values on which trust and respect can flourish. They include dedication and commitment, openness and candor, conflict resolution and crisis solving, creativity and innovation, and a host of others. Without these values present to provide for sound cooperation, other values step in to control: fighting, win/lose, exploitation, complacency, indifference, and even an atmosphere of sweetness and love that denies the existence of problems altogether. No amount of training in business practices or in problem solving suffices when the values that drive people are of this latter variety. With the former set of values in place, however, business practices and problem-solving skills find full and expressive use. This is why team building comes after value learning in Grid Organization Development. Without the foundation of learning gained in a Grid Seminar (whether acquired externally or in-house), teams are unable to grapple with significant value change. As a result, the contribution of a team-building exercise in terms of better performance is short-lived. With cooperation inside the corporation, the fullest effort can be aimed at outside competition rather than struggling among each other internally and dragging the organization down.

Conventional wisdom tells us there are three common efforts to shift culture, none of which seems very effective. One is prescription. The CEO (or a surrogate) tells the organization what is expected in the future. But it doesn't happen, at least not in any measurable way, and attention is diverted to new activities. A second is persuasion—encouraging change based on enthusiasm. It, too, is short-lived. A third is "natural spread." The CEO or leader substitute emphasizes what is being accomplished at some designated place, another company or even another country. People are sent to visit this location, with an expectation that they will return to implement what they have seen. More often than not, this proves to be a futile attempt at change.

The only approach that promises real change rests on helping people to think differently about themselves, their teams, and the organization as a whole. Such thinking must lead to convictions based on self-convincing personal evidence that comes to be widely shared with others.

Since Grid Organization Development (Grid OD) first evolved, a number of key changes have taken place. Although some of these are described in the basic texts, *The Managerial Grid III*[1] and *Grid IV*,[2] we have sought to include within this book the major points of application and implementation currently in use. Specific case studies are cited as a means for introducing the reader to the versatility of the Grid approach across a varied array of organizational cultures, both from a domestic and an international perspective. Although the basic phases of Grid OD itself have remained intact, they have also been enriched by the many new variations and extensions presented here. We have also outlined in detail for the first time our current approaches to organization diagnosis for determining the specific development needs of an organization and the process of setting in place a program for planned change.

Though there are other behavioral science–based approaches,

---

1.   Blake, R. R., and J. S. Mouton. 1985. *The Managerial Grid III*. Houston: Gulf Publishing.

2.   Blake, R. R., and J. S. Mouton. 1990. *The Managerial Grid IV*. Houston: Gulf Publishing.

no effort is made here to write a comparative treatment of OD. We have done this elsewhere.[3] Our purpose in this writing is to provide a full and comprehensive statement of one approach that has been tested and refined over a number of years. Although it is theoretical in formulation, it is thoroughly evaluated for effectiveness in actual practice.

Seven books mesh together in a usable way for anyone who wishes to deepen his or her conceptual and tactical understandings of this entire OD approach:

- *The Managerial Grid III* (1985) and *Grid IV* (1990, in press) identify the unsound and sound options for exercising problem-solving leadership.

- *Productivity: The Human Side* (1981) reviews the important facts about norms and standards and how to recognize them in order to change them.

- *Synergogy* (1984) describes the educational theory and practices we use to help any person or group of people learn the Grid theories, and evaluate and change their own leadership styles accordingly, and bring norms and standards to a manageable level where they can be changed.

- *Spectacular Teamwork* (1987) tells how to bring these leadership theories and sound norms and standards into use in one's own family work team.

- *Solving Costly Organizational Conflicts* (1984) depicts how to do so when conflict has become embedded at the interfaces that separate groups into competing components.

- *Consultation*, 2nd ed. (1983) is a comparative treatment of change strategies. It evaluates the strategies offered by others as a basis for open choice by the end users.

- *Change by Design* offers an overview as to how to institutionalize these numerous strategies in order to promote effectiveness throughout an entire organization.

Change by Design is organized in the following way. We begin

---

3. Blake, R. R., and J. S. Mouton. 1988. "Comparing Strategies for Incremental and Transformational Change." In *Corporate Transformation: Revitalizing Organizations for a Competitive World,* R. A. Kilmann and T. J. Covin, eds., San Francisco: Jossey-Bass, pp. 251–81.

with a case study of a change effort in a not-so-usual setting—the cockpit of the modern jet plane. The example serves to illustrate that "management problems" in the cockpit are not so very different than those that occur in the corporate boardroom. The Grid is introduced here in a specialized application. The dynamics of leadership evident within the story are apparent to anyone who works with and through others to achieve organization objectives.

Chapter 2 moves beyond a specific application and describes Grid theory in the context of the broader realm of today's organization—people managing people. Chapter 3 describes organization culture and outlines sound behavior dynamics requisite for mobilizing the wellsprings of human energy. Chapter 4 introduces our basic approaches to diagnosing the current state of organization health before proceeding to the next steps. Chapters 5 through 9 present the sequence of Grid OD, starting with Phase 1: The Managerial Grid Seminar, and continuing with Phase 2: Teamwork Development, Phase 3: Interface Conflict-Solving Model, Phase 4: Ideal Strategic Corporate Model, Phase 5: Implementation of the Ideal Model, and Phase 6: Stabilization and Consolidation of Progress before moving into another change cycle. Representative case studies are provided for each to illustrate the theory in real-life applications. A concluding chapter serves to summarize the implications presented in the book and to pose the challenge for OD in the years that lie ahead.

Dr. Jane Mouton died in December 1987, prior to completion of the final draft. The "we" or "us" used throughout the book generally refers to our joint activity, while the "I's" refer to one of us or another senior member of Scientific Methods, Inc., who carried out the activity reported here.

In an effort to fill the vacuum created by Jane's loss, Anne McCanse, having served as understudy to us both for the past fifteen years, stepped in to bring the manuscript through final draft and publication. She has done much to deepen the conceptual formulation, to make it sharper and more readable, and to include illustrations that give richer understanding to the message of the book.

Austin, Texas   Robert R. Blake
February 1, 1989   Anne Adams McCanse

Contents

1

Organization Change by Design

Work environments in virtually every industry and enterprise are often led by people who talk a big change game but don't actually play it. "We maximize our resources around here" is a vague statement that says, "What we do is good enough." The defensive posture that goes hand in hand with this is, "And, we can't do any better than this because of ... ." This latter statement quite often refers to *"them"*—bosses above, workers below, the union (or management), manufacturing (or sales), competitors, and so on. Seldom do people begin by looking in their own backyards for a solution to the problem of productivity and efficiency.

Organizational members may be divided into small groups and labeled "teams," and what they do may be called "teamwork" simply because they converse with one another on a regular basis. Such conversation may be of a social nature, a changing-of-the-guard or reporting of each person's piece of the action, or even cut-throat competition between individual soloists. Yet we are quick to call this teamwork, and it becomes acceptable to do nothing to promote anything other than what we are already doing.

The same is true of change. We may have instituted quality circle arrangements at one level of the organization. Our upper managers may roam the corporate halls, patting subordinates on the back (when they are caught doing something right) and saying, "Keep up the good work, whatever it is, whomever you are." We may send our managers to remote locations in search of greater productivity, requesting that they absorb the "how to's" and transplant them back at our home location. We may even set up giant corporate training centers, encouraging individual growth and development, all in the hope that the sum of each of these individual parts adds up to organizational change.

The concept of change denotes more than just the idea of improvement or incremental gain or even revolutionary turnaround or blind chance. It involves a great deal more than any of these. What we are talking about is change that goes to the heart of organization design and functioning. This is the focus of real change efforts and what we seek to accomplish through Grid Organization Development (Grid OD).

Real Change: Have We Got What It Takes?

When real change begins to take hold, there is no difficulty in recognizing it. The difficulty lies in seeing what makes it happen, what motivates organization members to surpass the ordinary and move into the realm of the extraordinary.

The idea of organization development—seeing the *organization,* not its individuals or teams, as the unit of change—is a turning point. Though the concept has been documented by many, awareness is growing of the precision required to bring about change in a deliberate and planned way.

Organization development comes in many shapes and forms, and it is difficult to point to features that the various approaches have in common. One distinct thread, however, is that whatever the approach, the objective is to improve human effectiveness in organized settings. Effectiveness means that objectives are being achieved in a cost-effective and humanly sound way; organized settings means that the effort is to increase effectiveness when more than one individual is involved.

An example of a change effort undertaken in such an organized setting, the goal of which was to increase flight safety effectiveness, is illustrated in the following case study:

> It looked as though all systems were go for United Airlines Flight 173, carrying eight crew members and 181 passengers on board, to make its descent into the Portland airport. Visibility and weather conditions were good; air traffic was not a problem; the flight was on schedule. Indeed, there was no reason to believe that all aboard the fated flight would not

soon be home with their families or departing for their next destination.

As the landing gear was lowered for touch-down, one of the three indicators failed to light, signaling that the gear had not locked in place. The captain quickly pulled out of the landing formation and proceeded to put the plane in a racetrack pattern while he and the first officer sought to determine where the malfunction lay. It could be the gear itself or it might just be a faulty light switch.

During this time, the second officer was keeping the crew apprised of the diminishing fuel situation, but the captain's focus remained centered on the equipment factor almost to the exclusion of the potential fuel dilemma. At one point, the captain requested that the second officer calculate fuel for another fifteen minutes, and the second officer replied, "Not enough." No further action was taken as attention was turned back to the equipment malfunction.

Approximately one hour after the initial landing attempt, all four engines suddenly ceased to operate and the plane dropped like a lead weight. As fortune would have it, the plane snagged on some electrical wires, which lessened the impact of the crash. Nonetheless, ten people on the aircraft died— eight passengers, a flight attendant, and, ironically, the second officer. In the aftermath, it was concluded that less than ten gallons of gas remained within the plane's tanks.

Definition of the Problem

The questions, of course, that first come to mind are, "How did such an accident occur?" and "Is there any way it could have been avoided?" Although an equipment malfunction of an undetermined nature was evident, other vital information was disregarded to the detriment of the well-being of the passengers and crew.

The National Transportation Safety Board (NTSB) reported that this accident is typical of many. They cited a breakdown in cockpit management and teamwork during a crisis situation. Specifically, the captain was so preoccupied with the landing gear problem that he failed to evaluate the impact of keeping the plane in a holding pattern despite diminishing fuel. Although the second officer sought to convey the impending danger to the captain, the intensity of focus on the equipment malfunction created tunnel vision, which excluded consideration of a potentially more volatile situation.

Typically, an airline examines the technical aspects for the cause of such an accident. However, advanced technology in the cockpit, along with the development of flight simulator training, has resulted in a high degree of reliability. Statistics show that few actual or potential aircraft accidents are due to equipment failure or lack of technical expertise on the part of the crew.

The welcome result of these technological breakthroughs has been an improvement in air flight safety. The piece of the puzzle that still eludes us, though, lies in the human factor—now attributed as the primary cause for most air accidents. In the period from 1970 to 1980, statistics reflected that 60 percent of all fatal commercial air carrier accidents were the result of poor management of the human resources available in the cockpit. If all the fatal accidents in the aviation industry (including corporate and general aviation) are examined for the same period, we find that 80 percent had this same mismanagement of resources as a causal factor. It is not surprising that the NTSB has pinpointed this as an area in need of improvement, emphasizing the absolute necessity of better management of available cockpit resources and more effective communication of vital information among crew members.

Ironically this is not so different from the situation confronting corporate executives. They come from similar backgrounds in terms of corporate culture. Both CEO and cockpit captain generally display strong leadership qualities, showing confidence in the strength of their convictions. Partly as a result of this very thinking, a new era of participative management has been ushered in, with a focus on synergistic teamwork in the work setting. Executives must learn to merge their own ideas with those of others in order to get the job done in a way that spells productivity for the corporation as a whole. It is evident that this cannot be achieved in a situation where everybody says "yes" to the boss or all are off doing their "own thing."

Based on the idea that if executives could undertake team-building steps to increase cooperation in the corporate setting, the same could be done in the cockpit, United Airlines (UAL) embarked on a project that pioneered a new training effort in the field of aviation. This thinking largely stemmed from the past experience of UAL management in Grid seminars where they had learned to recognize and avoid the very trap into which the crew of Flight 173 had fallen. This was, of course, a very innovative notion for any airline, where tradition dictates that if anything is wrong, the remedy lies in procedure, that is, throwing a checklist at it. Yet, it dug even deeper into the ingrained cockpit culture that said the captain was always right, no matter what, and that crew members functioned best when they buttoned their lips and did as they were told. The erroneous premise upon which the airline had been operating was that because a pilot had years of experience in a cockpit, he also possessed a high level of managerial expertise. The management task force therefore concluded, "The very advances in technology that have enhanced the safety of today's jet transport have led to a growing need for emphasis on the human side of flying. Today's pilot not only has to be a skilled aviator, but, just as important, must be skilled in working with others in effectively managing all crew resources."

Another task force was organized to investigate this problem of effectiveness. That union officers were included among this diagnostic body is particularly relevant. The significance of this step is that union members had the opportunity to participate from the ground level and could voice possible reservations during the design stage itself. Their support in implementing the final program was critical to its acceptance among the pilot population. Though other sources of tension had to be dealt with along the way, the basic intergroup aspect inherent in the union/management relationship did not prove to be an issue in the successful implementation of the approach. The widespread commitment and support from union membership stems primarily from the early involvement of the union. Management wasn't telling the union "what to do" in order to be more effective in the cockpit. Rather, union members were being given the chance to understand the underlying thinking behind the effort, and at the same time, the opportunity to offer input on potential solutions—it was a self-convincing approach.

We were solicited during this time to help the organization create a program that would resolve the safety problem. A committee was formed, composed of seven pilots on the one hand and seven applied behavioral scientists on the other. The charge was the design and development of materials for a captain's seminar. The committee was set up to meet for several week-long periods, with members then dispersing for back-home design and development. The group then reconvened to fine-tune the work done and to develop further ideas.

This notion of a joint task force turned out to be an excellent one, but it was not without its operational difficulties, particularly at the very beginning. Pilots themselves constitute an interesting group. They share an in-group culture, seeing themselves in a hardware world of nuts and bolts as defined by rigid requirements dictated from above. Partly due to this fact, they find communication with one another to be relatively easy but more difficult with strangers to their world. Furthermore we were perceived as people who dealt with such "soft" realities as human feelings—frustrations, tensions, hopes, and fears. Although these subjective elements were not under fire, they were, due simply to the nature of both groups, difficult to identify and deal with objectively.

Given these prevailing attitudes, the readiness for open, candid, freewheeling discussion of safety in the cockpit was somewhat limited. The early stages of discussion were distant and formal. Both sides seemed to be "feeling out" what was going on with the other, testing the potential for constructive collaboration. Only when the group decided to get down to practicalities did progress occur. The task force broke up into subgroups, approximately four members each, for the purpose of developing typical episodes, illustrating sound and unsound teamwork in the cockpit. The assignment was for the two pilots to write a first paragraph depicting the episode in a way that would illustrate a basic teamwork dynamic. Then the two behavioral experts were to write a second paragraph clarifying the underlying dynamics by providing the cause-and-effect aspects of the situation.

A real breakthrough to mutual respect between the two constituencies became apparent when pilots were called upon to agree or disagree with the analysis provided by the behavioral experts. In many cases, they were able to see it as "right on." In others, they were able to enrich the description based on their own experience. Conflict often led to new insight into the true dynamic underlying a situation, one that had not been evident to either party at the beginning of the discussion.

During our initial work, the captains had identified two key factors in the safety dilemma. One was "respect for captain authority," which, according to them, had been eroding since World War II. Their claim was that captains could no longer act with decisiveness and expect to receive anticipated compliance as had once been characteristic of the power and authority systems in place at an earlier time. The other factor involved cockpit discipline, that is, strengthening flying safety by operating the cockpit in conformance with procedures embedded in operations manuals, checklists, and so on. Both factors called for increased authority through greater decisiveness and better cockpit discipline, thus representing a shift in cockpit culture toward obedience norms as the basis for reinforcing leadership.

A number of activities were added to evaluate this assumption that an increase in captain's authority would show a decrease in pilot error and hence increased safety records. The result? Despite efforts to enhance the role of the captain and restore crew discipline, accident statistics remained static—for some reason, the problem persisted.

A central issue of effective transformation is valid diagnosis. The question now facing us was, "In the cockpit situation, had the real issue been addressed?" Change efforts based on a maldefinition of barriers to effectiveness or strategies for removing them do not bring about valid solutions, no matter how much energy and devotion may be applied. Therefore a series of experiments was conducted to test whether this assessment was on target or whether something entirely different might be involved.

A New Approach:
Challenging Conventional Wisdom

As progress was made in the task force, the original diagnosis based on strengthening captain authority and cockpit discipline was relinquished and a new and different understanding of the underlying dynamics came into view. This took place as the result of critique and diagnosis of the change effort as it was underway.

United Airlines had already begun to institute changes in technical procedures and crew selection. Our analysis began with a study of crew behavior, both in actual and in simulated flights. The objective was to develop a multifaceted, all-encompassing change strategy, one that would lead to improved problem solving and also would create an atmosphere of openness within the cockpit that could ensure a more efficient and safe operation.

The first step in the program was to provide crew members with an operational understanding of behavioral dynamics. The Managerial Grid[1] was used as the framework to bring about understanding and to provide a common "language" in the succeeding application phases of the program. The Grid itself is a framework on which different leadership approaches can be plotted against the criteria of *concern for performance* (that is, getting the job done) on the one hand and *concern for people* (that is, other crew members) on the other. Six basic leadership styles characterize crew interaction in the cockpit. The Grid, as adapted for the cockpit situation, is shown in Fig. 1–1.

Six styles of crew performance are important to the study and understanding of cockpit teamwork. The styles discussed here correspond to plots 9,1 1,9 1,1, 5,5, and 9,9 on the Grid. The numbers 1 and 9 symbolize *low and high degrees of concern and do not represent specific amounts.* The sixth style, paternalism, cannot be shown *physically* in the figure, but it represents a joining of the 9,1 and 1,9 styles. In Grid language, we can depict it as 9,1-1,9.

For example, a crew member with a high concern for performance (9) and a low concern for people (1) is denoted 9,1 on the Grid. This is the traditional authority-obedience basis of leadership. People are treated as tools of production that are used for successful task completion, not as potential resources that can enhance flight safety and problem resolution. In contrast, the 1,9 orientation focuses on good relations in the cockpit, to the possible detriment of safety. The rationale is that if crew members feel "comfortable" with one another, they naturally do everything possible to cooperate when called upon to do so. Right in the middle of this is the 5,5 approach, which says that a balance between these two extremes is the best that can be achieved. In many ways, this 5,5 orientation seemed to characterize the erosion of captain's authority and crew discipline that had taken place within the cockpit and was thought to be at the root of the "human factor" problem.

Even the 1,1 approach (low concern for safety and other crew members) is present in the cockpit. In fact, partly as a result of the existing seniority system for promoting individuals from the right seat to the left seat of a plane, some crew members "grow into" this role of doing the bare minimum and deferring to the captain's judgment rather than maintaining a critical, problem-solving attitude. According to one seasoned captain:

> Just as captains get stuck in their careers with no room for promotion, moreover, first officers frequently are entrapped by the seniority system and often spend years flying as No. 2. Some captains feel this undermines the system because the

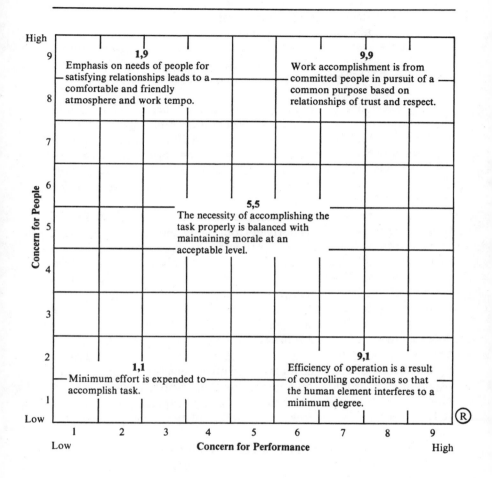

Figure 1–1
The Cockpit Grid®

Source: Blake, R. R., J. S. Mouton (Scientific Methods, Inc.), and Command/ Leadership/Resource Management Steering Committee and Working Groups (United Airlines). 1982. *Cockpit Resource Management.* Denver/Austin: Cockpit Resource Management. Reprinted with permission.

first officers become complacent and prefer to have the captain make the decisions. As one captain put it, 'After about three years in the copilot seat, most guys start to get numb above the shoulders. It takes a rare type of captain to push the thinking chores over to the right side of the airplane!'[2]

Paternalism represents a need to control, master, and dominate joined with displays of recognition and appreciation for compliance. A high concern for production (9,1) is coupled with a high concern for people (1,9) when desired results are achieved. The motivation is not only to retain control over others but to gain their admiration as well. When they resist, reprimands are relied on for getting people back into line.

A paternalist enjoys being the "expert," the one who "knows it all," and satisfaction is derived from being the source of wisdom to which others turn. When others accept the direction and guidance from the paternalistically oriented crew member, he or she feels warmth toward the team for its loyalty; but when they balk, this resistance is viewed as disloyalty and they may be deemed unworthy of deserving further assistance. Since there is a tendency for other crew members to remain dependent by yielding to the paternalist's wishes, crew members are prevented from growing and developing toward independence of thought, judgment, and convictions. Paternalistic behavior that discourages and often rejects the thinking and capabilities of other people generates frustration, resistance, and alienation. Crew members find it difficult to express these feelings to the paternalist who offers a sense of security for compliance with demands.

Finally, 9,9 (a full integration of both concerns) provides an option that might be expected to tap the available cockpit resources more effectively. The 9,9 orientation entails crew leadership based on involvement, participation, and commitment. It is not an abdication of responsibility on the part of the captain—in other words, by no means is the intent to diminish the captain's authority—however, the purpose is to open up the cockpit to the full contribution of members in order that all critical information can be present in the decision-making process.

Thus, in this way, the Grid provided a basis for examining each of these leadership styles within the cockpit, allowing those pilots who participated in the training experience to draw their own conclusions about the effectiveness of the various leadership approaches. Additionally this enabled us to test the conventional wisdom solution that increased captain authority would result in fewer pilot-error accidents (which had not proven to be the case) in order to gain insight on the true nature of the problem.

We designed a series of field experiments centered around in-flight dilemmas that had no previously programmed or "right" answers. Thus the thinking and judgment of flight crews, based on available resources, could be engaged in order to reach a solution.

At this point the client decided, despite our reservations, that only captains should participate in the learning experiments, a decision that later proved significant. Part of the client's reasoning behind this decision was that captains' authority might be further eroded if first and second officers observed captains handling dilemmas ineffectively. It appeared better for captains (at least from a personal point of view) to have the opportunity to explore their thinking and develop skills in dealing with a crisis interaction only in association with others of the same rank.

Hence, in the field research, captains were grouped randomly in three-person crews, with one designated as the captain in charge, the second as copilot (first officer), and the third as flight engineer (second officer). Thus all crew positions were covered, but the person sitting in the copilot's seat or the flight engineer's seat (in actuality, both captains themselves) might end up having more flying hours than the designated captain. They organized into crew formation and were provided certain specifications for the "leg" they were about to fly, say from New York to Los Angeles. Since this all took place in a conference room, the replication is of the human element, shorn of the high-tech aspects of the cockpit itself. The significance of this is derived from the distinct tendency to look to technology, or operations as a whole, whenever a problem arises, rather than to the potential human problems that could exist within that system. By creating simulations essentially free of such high-tech constraints, experimental crews were able to observe and experience just the human factor.

During the flight, a *planned dilemma* with no time for prior consideration was created for each crew. In this context, a dilemma is a problem to be solved, but for which no standard solution has been established from an operations manual or elsewhere. The dilemma is separated into three parts, with each crew member designation receiving a specified piece of information. An example of one such dilemma follows.

Dilemma A³

Scenario Provided to "Captain"

You are a crew member on a westbound flight between two airports located 800 miles apart. Your destination airport has an elevation of 1025 feet MSL. About 30 minutes east of your destination, you receive a call from the company notifying you of a bomb threat. The company indicated that the caller sounded very knowledgeable. The bomb is said to be an aneroid-type detonation device set for 6000 MSL and the threat, therefore, is that the bomb will explode should you descend below 6000 MSL. The caller indicated that the bomb was located in a part of the aircraft inaccessible to you but would not say where. The caller further indicated that there was a note in a forward lavatory explaining why the bomb had been placed on board. The crew has investigated in the cabin and the note cannot be located.

The company engineering department has calculated your fuel burnout using the most economical cruise available to you and has determined that if you maintain cruise as long as possible and then drift down, you would still be thirty miles short of an airport located west of your destination in the foothills of a high mountain range with a field elevation of 6172 feet MSL. This is the closest airport above 6000 feet available to you.

Scenario Provided to "First Officer"

You are a crew member on a westbound flight between two airports located 800 miles apart. Your destination airport has an elevation of 1025 feet MSL. About 30 minutes east of your destination, you receive a call from the company notifying you of a bomb threat. The company indicated that the caller sounded very knowledgeable. The bomb is said to be an aneroid-type detonation device set for 6000 MSL and the threat, therefore, is that the bomb will explode should you descend below 6000 MSL. The caller indicated that the bomb was located in a part of the aircraft inaccessible to you but would not say where. The caller further indicated that there was a note in a forward lavatory explaining why the bomb had been placed on board. The crew has investigated in the cabin and the note cannot be located.

The company engineering department has calculated your fuel burnout using the most economical cruise available to you and has determined that if you maintain cruise as long as possible and then drift down, you would still be thirty miles short of an airport located west of your destination in the foothills of a high mountain range with a field elevation of 6172 feet MSL. This is the closest airport above 6000 feet available to you.

During your career, you have been involved in one other bomb threat that was somewhat different since it was not an aneroid-type detonator nor did it include a note. This previous threat proved to be untrue. You are also very much aware that there are inherent discrepancies in aircraft fuel gauges. Therefore, due to the uncertainty of fuel and the great probability that the bomb threat is untrue, you feel the wisest course of action would be to land at your original destination. You feel there are greater risks to your life and those of other crew members and passengers should an attempt be made to proceed to the higher elevation airport, since there are no suitable airports for your aircraft type, regardless of field elevation, along your route for about 400 n.m. east of that airport.

Scenario Provided to "Second Officer"

You are a crew member on a westbound flight between two airports located 800 miles apart. Your destination airport has an elevation of 1025 feet MSL. About 30 minutes east of your destination, you receive a call from the company notifying you of a bomb threat. The company indicated that the caller sounded very knowledgeable. The bomb is said to be an aneroid-type detonation device set for 6000 MSL and the threat, therefore, is that the bomb will explode should you descend below 6000 MSL. The caller indicated that the bomb was located in a part of the aircraft inaccessible to you but would not say where. The caller further indicated that there was a note in a forward lavatory explaining why the bomb had been placed on board. The crew has investigated in the cabin and the note cannot be located.

The company engineering department has calculated your fuel burnout using the most economical cruise available to you and has determined that if you maintain cruise as long as possible and then drift down, you would still be thirty miles short of an airport located west of your destination in the foothills of a high mountain range with a field elevation of 6172 feet MSL. This is the closest airport above 6000 feet available to you.

Your experience as a crew member tells you that a crew can usually improve on the planned fuel burnout. Therefore you believe that good use of resources by the crew will make it possible for the aircraft to reach the higher elevation airport. Since you are uncertain about the bomb and have strong feelings that it would be possible to make the airport to the west by wise usage of fuel, you feel very strongly that the flight should proceed to that airport. In addition, you have been closely monitoring fuel consumption and know that the aircraft has been consuming less fuel than the flight plan predicted. You firmly believe this burnout trend will continue to happen.

The dilemma activity met with a wide variation in results. Roughly one-third of the crews passed with flying colors; another third encountered difficulty; and the final third failed to complete the task in an acceptable manner. It is important to note that all crews were composed solely of captains. Over the course of the trial runs, every captain had the opportunity to experience the handling of dilemmas from each cockpit position.

Upon completion of a trial run, members of each crew evaluated how well they had dealt with the dilemma. Though some crews felt satisfied with their performance, what became clear to many who operated in the first and second officer roles was that they felt resentful of the manner in which the designated captain had handled the problem. The Seminar Manager reassembled teams into groups of three and asked them, "How well do you feel you handled the dilemma as a crew?"

First Officer: Well, I'm angry! I had a really good solution for dealing with the problem, but I couldn't get a word in edgewise. (*Turning to captain*) You never even asked me what I thought.

Captain: I assumed you agreed with the decision I made.

First Officer: I never had a chance. You told me what to think and what to do. I resent being treated like a machine.

Captain: I'm sorry. You should have said something. I had no idea ...

Second Officer: I feel the same way. There were a lot of options we failed to look at and there was plenty of time. But you honed in on your own interpretation of the situation and left us out completely. We made it back, but it was by the skin of our teeth. Personally, I prefer a wider safety margin.

First Officer: Yeah, we lucked out. I'd think twice before making that decision again.

The designated captains were dumbfounded. Suddenly they realized that resources had been present and that time had been available—and yet they failed to use these resources. Instead, they relied on their own thinking to the exclusion of the thinking of others of equal training and experience, to say nothing of equal time in the left seat. When this kind of episode was repeated again and again, the evidence became self-convincing indeed, not only to those pilots who were designated captains but to those captains who were flying in subordinate crew positions as well. The latter came to realize that they, too, were part of the problem. They had had an opportunity to express their convictions, but for the most part they had failed to do so, particularly when the designated captain presented a forceful position. They had begrudgingly submitted instead of advocating their own positions, which may have provided sounder courses of action.

The tendency was for the captain to centralize authority to the exclusion of input from the first and second officers, falling back on a compliance-based style of leadership that dictated what others were to do without question. The crew complied but their resentment was revealed in the critique discussions that followed. When the

Captain directs execution by
others who passively comply;
one-way input—top down.

Figure 1–2
The Pre-Training Conception of Human Resource Utilization in the Cockpit

captain centralized authority in this way, as shown in Fig. 1–2, input by other crew members was effectively shut out. Critical information was left unexamined and potential solutions therefore remained unidentified. Flight 173 illustrates the problem. The second officer warns the captain of the low fuel situation, but the captain takes no heed of the input provided. The result? A crash due to "insufficient fuel" to complete the landing.

In the dilemma activities, time was available to share and exchange ideas, and most crew members became convinced that effective use of all available resources within the cockpit, that is, maximizing the contributions of all three "experts," would have resulted in better solutions with less risk to life and limb.

A dramatic illustration is provided in an NTSB memorandum on how a Cockpit Resource Management (Grid) trained crew dealt with a wind shear event on leaving Denver's Stapleton Airport as contrasted with a second crew not trained in similar Grid principles.

> On May 31, 1984, at 1334 mountain daylight time, United Airlines Flight 663, a Boeing 727-222, N7647U, departed Denver, Colorado, for Las Vegas, Nevada, with 98 passengers and 7 crew members on board. At that time, wind shear was being reported at Denver's Stapleton International Airport with the centerfield wind from 280 degrees at 22 knots,

gusting to 34 knots. During the takeoff from runway 35L, the aircraft lost 20 knots of airspeed at rotation and used almost the entire length of the runway to reach its takeoff and climb speed. However, almost immediately after it began its climb, the aircraft struck the localizer antenna located 1074 feet beyond the end of the runway at a height of 15 feet above the ground. No one was hurt as a result, but the aircraft fuselage was damaged substantially. The aircraft climbed to 10,000 feet altitude before the crew realized that the cabin could not be pressurized. The crew returned to Denver, landing the aircraft without incident.

On June 13, 1984, at 1656 eastern daylight time, USAir Flight 183, from Hartford, Connecticut, a DC9-31, N964VJ, with 50 adult passengers, 1 infant passenger, and 5 crew members crashed at Detroit Metropolitan Airport while attempting a go-around following an instrument landing system (ILS) approach to runway 21R. Although no one was killed in the crash, five persons were injured, and the aircraft was damaged substantially. At the time of the accident, there was heavy rain, hail, and low-level wind shear reported at the airport.

In both these accidents, transport category aircraft encountered wind shear after air traffic controllers transmitted wind shear reports in conditions in which there was a high probability of wind shear encounter ... .

The flightcrews of the aircraft reacted differently to the respective hazardous situation they each faced. The second officer on United Flight 663, according to the crew members' statements, strongly asserted, "Captain, you've lost 20 knots of airspeed." The captain immediately advanced the throttles to their mechanical limits and adjusted the aircraft pitch attitude to reduce to a minimum any decrease in the initial climb rate. These timely actions were critical in preventing a more severe accident and a potential catastrophe.

The flightcrew of USAir Flight 183 was unsure of the winds, which exceeded the carrier's DC9 crosswind landing limitations and failed to ask for clarification on the nature of the winds. According to the cockpit voice recorder transcript, there was no discussion initiated by either crew member on the need for more current wind or visibility information or on the possibility of discontinuing the approach and initiating a go-around ... .

In a wind shear environment, immediate access by flight crew members to wind data is particularly critical since wind shear is such a dynamic phenomenon where conditions can change rapidly and dramatically. The Safety Board recognizes that despite the variety of information available to pilots on the presence of wind shear, none offers a precise measurement of the hazards that pilots can expect to encounter. As a result, pilots in command must make the most prudent decision possible, using all available information, on the advisability of conducting a flight into a wind shear environment. There are no absolute standards available to crew members, such as there are for prevailing visibility for example, that will categorically permit or prohibit a takeoff or a landing ... .

Both flightcrews received training that met or exceeded Federal Aviation Regulations, but they reacted and performed differently in the accident sequences. The Safety Board realizes that any number of variables can affect pilot behavior and performance. For example, the second officer on United Flight 663 is a management pilot who is a B-727-rated captain and check airman, as well as a rated flight engineer. His role with the company could account for both his assertiveness in the cockpit and the captain's immediate and positive response to his call-out.

Another factor that could account for the difference in response is the difference in cockpit resource management training that the two carriers offer their crews. Cockpit resource management refers to the use of all flightcrew members to enhance pilot decision making, communication, crew interaction, and crew integration. USAir currently offers captains who have been upgraded to that position recently a two-day classroom-type session in human relations. Other crew members do not receive this type of training. United requires all crew members to receive formal cockpit resource management training, both initial and recurrent, involving classroom as well as simulator session ... .

The Safety Board believes that United's cockpit resource management training may have played a positive role in preventing a more serious accident from occurring in Denver and that it is an endeavor that should be encouraged. The Board previously has recognized the benefits of this training when it recommended in 1979, as the result of several accident investigations in which the breakdown in cockpit resource management was identified as a contributing factor, that the FAA:

> Urge ... operators to ensure that their flightcrews are indoctrinated in principles of flight deck resource management, with particular emphasis on the merits of participative management for captains and assertiveness training for other cockpit crew members.(A-79-47)[4]

Time after time the captains had responded to crises with the traditional pattern of centralizing authority that is consistent with the earlier research findings based on the 9,1 authority-obedience premise. The designated captains were able to arrive at decisions with no cases of insubordination or panic by crew members. But, when it came to assessing the *quality* of the solution, in two-thirds of the trials, something else became dramatically apparent. The second and third crew members turned to the captain and said, in effect, "If you had consulted us, we could have given you information that would have enabled you to take a better action than you took." They had missed *sounder* solutions because crew members had been given little opportunity to provide necessary data. In cases where input of a problem-solving nature had been offered, it had not been "heard." The participants in these experiments went on to discuss alternative possibilities, and captain after captain became aware of how conventional behavior had prevented them from tapping available resources before deciding which course of action to implement.

Since all members of the critique were captains, the final assessment had special impact. The designated captain could not say, "The copilot is just sore because he hasn't made it to the left seat, and he probably never will," or "The second officer doesn't know what it's like to sit in my seat and be responsible for the lives of 400 people." These rationalizations were successfully eliminated because the learning experiment crews were composed exclusively of peers.

These experiments led to fundamental reevaluations about safety in emergency or crisis situations. The pilots learned from experience that they were failing to recognize that others have knowledge and may be able to contribute to a valid and safe resolution of a crisis. Additionally they learned that when there is sufficient time to do otherwise but the captain nevertheless centralizes authority, this in effect shuts out information others are capable of contributing. An approximate redefinition of the problem came to be recognized by the experimental captain group:

> At the point when crises appear, even though sufficient time is available for finding a solution, the overriding tendency is for captains to centralize authority within themselves and to command the solution to be implemented. The time available between recognition of the existence of a problem and the implementation of a solution is ample for crew consultation, review, and critique, but the step involving crew input is bypassed. In bypassing these steps, the available input from one or two other experienced flying personnel is sacrificed. The practical effect of this is that only one-third or possibly one-half (in two-person crews) of the available technical understanding of how to solve the problem is brought into use.

This is exemplified in the following illustration.[5]

Captain: Gear up.

(*During climbout, the firebell and wheel-well fire light that is next to the number three engine fire switch illuminates.*)

Captain (to the copilot): You've got the airplane; I'll take care of the fire.

Flight Engineer: It's a wheel-well fire. (*The bell is silenced.*)

Captain (radio): Universal 123 returning to land. We have a fire.

Tower: Roger, Universal 123. Turn to 090. Maintain 7000. You'll be number one for 26 left.

(As the copilot looks out the right window to clear for the turn, the captain pulls the number three engine fire handle.)

Flight Engineer: Now we have number three shut down and we still have the wheel-well fire.

The captain disregarded input from the flight engineer in identifying the difficulty. The captain jumped to a conclusion and took unilateral action. If he had had a different attitude toward utilizing crew resources he would have checked before taking action, or at the very least might have been alert to the flight engineer's remarks. The result might have been that a relatively simple situation would not have been compounded.

Another example follows:

(Flight 798 is heading east on a radar vector for landing at San Diego. Weather at San Diego is 3000 overcast, 8 miles visibility, wind 270 degrees at 7 knots.)

Copilot: They ought to be letting us down pretty soon.

Captain: That controller will probably jam all the arrivals from the east in front of us. We'll have plenty of time to get down.

Approach Control: Universal 798, turn right to heading 180, descend to 4000 feet, cleared for the back course approach to runway 27. Contact the tower now 124.7.

Copilot: Roger, San Diego Tower. Universal 798.

Copilot: Wonder exactly how far out we are?

San Diego Tower: Universal 798 is cleared to land. Wind 270 at 7.

Copilot: Roger, Universal 798 is cleared to land runway 27.

Copilot: We're awfully close in.

Captain: Just put the gear down and run the list. We're breaking out now. I can see the runway.

Copilot: It sure doesn't seem like a west wind up here.

Captain: Flaps 2.

Copilot: We are still a little fast for 2.

(Captain reaches across and puts the flaps to 2.)

Copilot: Our usual turn around the hospital will give us the room we need.

Captain: Flaps 5.

Copilot: We're still a little fast, but your speed is starting to come down.

(Captain reaches across and selects flaps 5.)

(Captain reaches across and selects flaps 25.)

Copilot: These flaps take forever when you need them.

Captain: Especially if you delay them. There is considerable margin built into the design that you sometimes have to take advantage of.

(Captain reaches across and selects flaps 30.)

Copilot: You're going to get the Ground Proximity Warning because your sink is 1800. Do you think ... Ah ... maybe we ought to ...

(After touchdown, 3500 feet down the runway, Universal 798 is able to stop near the far end by heavy use of brakes and reverse.)

Tower: Universal 798, you have smoke coming from your gear. Do you need equipment?

The captain's centralization of authority is first seen in the manner in which he handles input from the copilot. None of the clues put before him that the approach is deteriorating sway him from his strong conviction. He develops tunnel vision and nothing is going to deter him from doing it his way. He personally takes actions when the copilot hesitates. His responses to the copilot's weak attempts to point out the problem are caustic comments. Had the captain been sensitive to the copilot's advocacy, weak as it was, he would have been aware of the deterioration of the approach and could have taken corrective action.

These findings were at odds with the preliminary interview-based conclusions. The issues are not "respect for captain authority" or "cockpit discipline." Rather, they are ones of opening the cockpit to fuller participation in order to mobilize the resources that other crew members can contribute. An entirely different formulation of the problem comes into view: "How can cockpit leadership be experienced to bring forth collaborative use of resources in the interest of safe flying?" This is the confrontation approach to conflict resolution with the captain becoming accessible to the potential contributions of colleagues in an atmosphere reinforced by norms of openness and candor. This 9,9 leadership model is shown in Fig. 1–3.

The insight is basic. Although there can be no doubt that the captain is in charge and maintains responsibility for reaching the ultimate decision, one key to increased safety lies in keeping the crisis situation open to interaction as long as possible or necessary rather than shutting it down. It is critical for the captain (or any executive, manager, or supervisor) to keep information flowing back and forth instead of issuing arbitrary commands to "do this" or "do that."

Although insufficient time is often used to justify the centralization of authority—whether in the cockpit or in the boardroom—it is, in fact, only a rare case where time is actually too limited to tap into other resources. Whether one minute or thirty, there usually exists sufficient time to permit input that could make a vital difference.

Again, think of Flight 173. Had the captain acknowledged the fuel shortage dilemma and instructed the second officer to calculate the remaining time and options available, the situation might have been rectified. The tragedy was not a function of lack of time, but rather one of poor use of time. As a team they might have discussed the implications of potential problems and determined actions to be taken—making sound decisions based on the information they did

Captain leads decision making
based on full human resource
utilization; interactive exchanges.

Figure 1–3
The Post-Training Conception of Human Resource Utilization in the Cockpit

know, delegating responsibility to each member to seek answers to what they didn't know, and setting in place a deadline for when some specified action must take place in order to avoid crisis.

With this redefined diagnosis of the problem, it was possible to move forward in design and development work and effectively to create what has become the basic structure of Cockpit Resource Management.

Change Crew Behavior, Not Just Captain Behavior

Another aspect of the systematic research related to the conventional wisdom hypothesis about crisis management needs to be brought into focus. As mentioned earlier, expectations that the person in charge assumes command and control are as deeply embedded in the life experiences of other crew members as they are in the designated leader. In a crisis situation, not only do members wait for the person in charge to initiate action with little or no expectation of being involved in diagnosis about the best thing to do, but they tend to be less assertive and more deferent to the leader. That is, they are even more likely to withhold critical information if the leader does not seek and draw out these resources. The quality of leadership becomes central at this point.

Findings from research in small group crisis solving have substantiated this tendency to withdraw. These are revealed in the following key points:

1. When three (or more) people of equal rank meet with crisis, there is widespread reluctance for any member to exercise initiative. Reluctance increases with the size of the group at least up to six people and probably beyond.[6,7]

2. When one person is placed in charge, that person tends to assume responsibility and to step forward and exercise full initiative.[8]

3. When the person in charge exercises such initiative, others adopt a passive, follow-the-leader orientation.[9,10]

4. When the person in charge seeks to solve the crisis, he or she does so directly by telling others what to do.[11]

5. Centralizing authority in himself or herself, the person in charge effectively shuts out useful input from others.[12]

6. Those not in charge are reluctant to speak up even when they disagree with the high risk behavior of the person in charge, thereby shutting themselves out of the problem-solving loop.[13]

7. Points 4, 5, and 6 become stronger when the competence of the person in charge has been demonstrated previously.[14]

These findings lead to strong conclusions. The issue is not merely that of lodging authority in the single person who is in charge and therefore in control. The necessity for that is taken for granted, in line with avoiding the adverse implications of point 1. The problem, rather, is the manner in which that person exercises his or her vested authority. The conventional manner for taking charge and directing action, without consulting others as to their diagnoses or recommendations, has the effect of shutting out potentially valuable input that they may be in a position to provide, in line with points 2–6. If that input is needed but unavailable and the leader has the wrong concept of the problem to be solved or of the best option for solving it, the results can lead to tragic consequences. By com-

The 10:00 culture based on top down, one-way communication.

Figure 1–4
The Pre-Training Cockpit Culture

parison, the issue is *full* use of all available resources, technical and human, prior to decision making.

Points 2–7 currently prevail as the basis for handling many cockpit crises. It is in that context that the operation of points 3–7 is inappropriate and potentially hazardous.

The exercise of authority and the norms and standards inherent in the cockpit culture seem congruent with these findings. We can portray them graphically to better understand how this development project unfolded. Prior to the training intervention, we can say that all the crew members operated according to a ten o'clock point of view, with ten o'clock used symbolically to convey the shared expectations about centralizing captain authority and passive response norms that prevailed among other crew members. This shared norm is shown in Fig. 1–4.

By contrast, after training on a captain-only basis, captains had learned the soundness of a two o'clock culture for crisis management; that is, a culture in which consultation and critique precedes decision making. Many of the captains in the field test returned to the line with a fundamental commitment to change, convinced that a two o'clock way of conducting the cockpit was the sounder approach. They sought to implement dynamic leadership according to the conventional approach of bringing about improvement, that is, they "intuitively" selected modeling as the way to promote the

Culture clash when the captain
has embraced a 2:00 concept of
communication but the crew
remains committed to a 10:00
"tell me" orientation.

Figure 1–5
*The Contradiction Created by Individual Development in an
Organization Setting*

desired behavior. In effect, they said, "The way to get better cockpit performance is for me to act differently, to open the situation up, and to let crew members experience the benefits of greater participation in cockpit problem diagnosis." What happened when captains had a new view of how to exercise power and authority and the importance of the openness and candor norm, but first and second officers still did not? The result can be seen as in Fig. 1–5.

When the first problem arose, the captain said, "Look, this is not routine. The instruments are giving contradictory readings. What's going on here? Do you think we have a problem?" The idea was that such openness would bring forth an immediate and spirited response from other crew members, but this was not the case. Instead, crew members said to themselves, "We're really in a pickle! We have a potential crisis on our hands, and the captain doesn't know what to do!" The crew continued to operate according to the ten o'clock norm (waiting for the captain to take charge), while, as perceived by them, the captain was acting in a contradictory and incomprehensible way.

After a period of time, captains concluded that the two o'clock way of mobilizing resources was sound on paper and even produced better results in the field trials, but that it was simply impractical for use in routine flying. The result was that they shifted their reliance back to centralized captain authority.

A significant factor has been revealed in the preceding discussion. If all cockpit crew members do not understand the importance of open interchange, their expectations are shaken. That is, if a captain seeks to open the cockpit to crew member input and turns to them for input on a solution, this may be interpreted as uncertainty, weakness, or indecisiveness, thus increasing the level of confusion or chaos. This was the same basic insight that led to the emergence of organization development when the Grid framework was first set into place more than twenty-five years ago.[15] The point is that whenever a norm or standard of conduct is shared, the problem of change ceases to be an individual matter. It becomes a group or organizational issue. Ideally all norm-carriers have to be involved in changing the norms by which they have previously interacted with one another.

In the cockpit example, even though captains who had completed the training became convinced that the two o'clock method for management of resources was sound, they later concluded it would not work during routine flying. What they were really saying was something like, "The first and second officers misunderstand my openness. They think I am weak and are therefore anxious about my leadership." In other words, crew members were acting according to a norm of centralized authority, while the captain had been trying to exercise a new norm of participation. As a result of the "culture clash," captains abandoned their convictions about the soundness of a two o'clock way of operating in the cockpit and once again embraced the ten o'clock thesis.

The thinking that emerged was that participants needed the opportunity to reach a consensus on what was being learned, thereby establishing shared norms. Such episodes demonstrated that it was critical for *all* crew members to engage in the dilemma-solving training so as to create a common way of thinking about how best to mobilize cockpit resources.

This solution turned out to be consistent with organization development principles. It was imperative for all crew members to gain insight into the same set of management concepts in order to implement them effectively. As a result of recommendations to management from the test seminars, all of United's cockpit crew members participated in the training endeavor. Furthermore, the same framework is used as the basis for annual recurrent training among flight personnel.

Through the implementation, rather than elimination, of consultation and critique, an entirely new cockpit atmosphere began to emerge. It was an atmosphere in which the flying of the airliner or corporate aircraft became the joint responsibility of the crew, not some additive combination of two or three crew members, each conducting part of the job description and in their totality constituting the basis of flight performance. Rather, the cockpit atmosphere was to be an interactive one in which pilot A exercised initiative within his or her job description but also maintained a proactive orientation for how the other members were performing. This meant that pilot B could identify and thereby bring attention to some omission on the part of pilot A that had implications in terms of effectiveness. When pilots A, B, and C were all acting interdependently in this way, they could benefit from the additional observation, thought, and critique on the manner in which they were conducting the flight operation.

The implication for cultural change is depicted in the song of an earlier year, "It Takes Two to Tango." If both partners don't know the tune and the rhythm of the dance, there is no possibility of success.

The Rediscovery of OD

The organization development principle that had been clearly identified was that all who participate in carrying out an activity must necessarily share similar values and therefore contribute behavior consistent with those values in order for effective performance to result. Otherwise, it has been shown that when one member of a working party embraces certain values that are unrecognized by others with whom he or she must cooperate, one of several things is bound to happen. The person whose values are contradictory either chooses to leave the situation or else slowly but surely comes to accept the values embraced by the others, given that the others refuse to reverse their points of view. When a person has learned something of a value-relevant nature in a training or development environment, this new value or concept, if ignored or contradicted by others in the workplace, is abandoned in the interest of moving forward. This portrays the well-known phenomenon of fadeout. The unfortunate consequence is that old values that may be obsolete and even counterproductive are retained.

The cockpit example has been presented in detail because it clearly illustrates a major Grid OD change effort. These issues of effectiveness are by no means unique or limited to the cockpit example. Indeed, they are essentially identical to organization development insights that fell into place thirty years ago in change experiments undertaken at Exxon.[16] Top managers attended behavioral learning seminars and then returned to their work environments stimulated by the relevant discoveries and committed to introducing the changes that the new information had brought into focus for them. However, those in the workplace, unfamiliar with these new concepts and values, were unwilling to cooperate, seeing the changes as either trivial or insignificant, or more often repudiating them as impractical and unworkable. Whatever the immediate reaction, the new ideas were not subject to thoughtful and open review. It is interesting to speculate why.

Part of the reason is that people prefer to do what they have done in the past. This can be true even if historical limitations and deficiencies are openly acknowledged and even disparaged. This is often called "resistance to change" as though it were some inviolable human principle, even when people have experienced the very opposite condition: enthusiasm for change. What lies behind this apparent contradiction?

Part of the answer is that people engaged in a joint activity need a basis for shared understanding of the concepts and values underlying that activity. Then, these concepts and values can be contrasted with others in order to choose those that are most effective for the coordinated effort. This is at the very heart of organization development effectiveness. When this principle is ignored, the almost inevitable consequence is resistance to change. In reality this means nothing more than resistance due to ignorance; the solution is to provide insight that can replace the blind and mechanical acceptance of the past.

One further aspect is of critical importance. The concepts and insights we refer to need to be made available on a shared basis, not just provided to each individual independently of the others. In other words, the premise cannot be made that each individual, given the requisite insights and skills, automatically collaborates with others in their application. Effective interaction, a skill in itself, is essential to sound joint effort. The attainment of such skill is by no means difficult, and the educational methodologies for bringing effective interaction into use have long since been worked out and perfected.

We regard this project as a prototype of one important way of dealing with fundamental change. The same kinds of problems that exist in the cockpit are present in the executive suite,[17] on the shop floor,[18] in academic institutions,[19] and throughout the manufacturing and service industries.

One of the significant offshoots from the cockpit application is in the field of medicine where claims of malpractice are commonly the result of poor teamwork.[20] The care provided during and shortly after the birth of an infant is a medical management issue frequently examined in the courts. In fact, the legal liability in obstetrics has reached such magnitude that many physicians are leaving the specialty. Within the field of medicine, it has been concluded that physicians who stay and get caught up in claims of malpractice are oftentimes not negligent. The more common problem is that they are engaged in a rapidly changing field without the skills of coordination or cooperation that real teamwork makes possible.

A common illustration can be seen when an unborn baby begins to show signs of distress in labor and delivery. Due to communication channels previously established by the doctor, the nurse may or may not feel comfortable offering an opinion on the matter. For example, if the doctor is functioning as an overbearing "Captain of the Ship," the nurse may be relegated to the role of observer—while the patient's condition continues to deteriorate. While awaiting the doctor's decision as to a course of action, for example, in a cesarean section, the nurse may dutifully record the chain of transpiring events but offer nothing in terms of input. Poor time management and inadequate use of resources, that is, the nurse's expertise, may lead to what could have been a preventable situation. When the pediatrician is finally called into the picture, the interaction becomes even more complex. Because preplanning was bypassed and time pressures became compelling, the communication that needed to take place between members of the medical team was absent or provided only in a secondhand way. Quite often, the end result is further miscommunication and potentially life-threatening mistakes.

Calling the pediatrician into labor and delivery with no prior warning of a possible problem is a classic demonstration of the lack of teamwork, often leading to a poor outcome for the infant. If problems have arisen, but the obstetrician has failed to alert the pediatrician to potential complications, a serious injury to the infant can result in the first few minutes of life. The ensuing debate between doctors focuses on whether the pediatrician complied with a standard requiring immediate availability in case of emergency or whether instead the obstetrician was negligent for not having called the pediatrician earlier. The nurse, who plays a central position, may have been ignored completely. Undoubtedly the nurse could have coordinated team effort by offering to do so and/or making the required phone call, but the traditional role does not support the taking of such initiative.

Problems of teamwork also appear in the emergency room and surgical amphitheater. For example, a surgeon can be so caught up in the technical aspects of a difficult operation that excessive blood loss on the part of a patient goes unnoticed. If the anesthesiologist fails to mention this fact until trouble is encountered with inadequate blood pressure, it is slightly akin to an airliner running out of fuel at 30,000 feet. At this point, the patient goes into shock; very few options remain to be exercised. Seeking to complete the procedure may result in further blood loss. Subsequent blood transfusions are risky in that they may leave the patient with hepatitis or AIDS. In other words, it is a far better option not to allow the patient's condition to deteriorate to this point. The worst outcome, other than death, may find the patient on a respirator awaiting diagnosis as to extent of brain damage. A claim of negligence in such a case is extremely hard to defend.

What we are dealing with here is a group of people—*not a team*. Each individual is well trained, but the resulting decisions made independently tend to treat only that part of the problem that fits into each specific speciality. The concept of preplanning has been replaced by assumptions that say, "I am an expert and don't need to coordinate with others as long as these other professionals, whom I presume are also experts, do their jobs right." When complications do arise, the back-up assumption is, "Call in another specialist." This may in turn lead to further complications, and so on down the line. Because of the crisis in malpractice litigation, this type of poor teamwork is finally emerging as an issue that will grow more significant and complex with further advances in technology until it is effectively resolved.

The same issues can be seen on the nuclear plant floor where high-tech considerations are ineffectively dealt with by low-tech applications of power and authority.[21] The nuclear operator is a member of a dynamic profession. The technology, environment, and very nature of operations seem to be in a constant state of change. Although it is relatively easy to identify significant shifts in plans or procedures, it is much more difficult to assess specific changes that occur in the human side of productivity. Operator training historically has focused on operating skills and systems knowledge, while neglecting or ignoring such factors as how control room operators communicate and the effective sharing of relevant information that takes place in the process of decision making.

In an emergency, conventional wisdom commends an authoritarian leadership style; take over, designate who is to do what, and command the implementation. The person in charge acts decisively by detailing exactly how the problem is to be approached and who is to do what. In an uncomplicated operation, the cause of a problem is expected to be self-evident. In this case, it takes no great analytical skill on the part of the supervisor to see what the problem is and how it should be handled. Whether there might be a better approach is not open to question. This rational prescription assumes that the supervisor knows how to orchestrate and delegate the right mix of skills so that the work gets accomplished. But it remains a one-person show with many hands implementing the commands.

In a more complicated operation, direct perception can no longer be relied on as the basis for identifying the cause of the problem. An environment of control panels, analog and/or digital monitors, and other instruments does not permit a hands-on approach. The person in charge often relies on readings or judgments by others who are in physical proximity to the data. Computations must be made, inferences drawn, and conclusions derived.

It follows that a crisis solution in an uncomplicated operation cannot extend to a more complicated problem. Data from the nuclear power industry, called significant operating experience reports, point to the same conclusion: the absence of teamwork. The following example portrays this traditional approach to leadership in the nuclear plant control room:

> The plant has just completed a short outage and is finishing the final check-off to change from Shutdown to Startup modes. Bill, the shift supervisor, is determined to make the mode change on his shift. The control room operator, Joe, is performing the final checks on the auxiliary feedwater system.

"Hey, Joe, what's the holdup? I want to get that mode change in on our shift."

"I'm just trying to do it right, and it looks like we may have a problem here."

"Oh, come on," Bill smirks, "You're always looking for something to hold us up. What is it now?"

"The auxiliary feed pump discharge temperature is reading higher than normal."

"Come on, Joe, it always reads high. I think you're just trying to slow things down again."

Jim, the reactor operator, has been listening to all of this and comes to the defense of Joe. "Hey, Bill, that's not fair. Joe is just trying to do his job. Besides, just because it has read high in the past doesn't mean that it's all right now."

"Why don't you just stay out of this," replies Bill in a superior tone. "I'm sure there's no problem. Let's just get the damn checklist done and worry about the temperature later."

Joe goes ahead and completes the checklist, still not sure that the temperature is correct. "You know, Jim, I still think Instruments & Controls should check out that temperature and make sure it's okay."

"I don't know," Jim answers. "Bill seems pretty sure that there's no problem and he is the shift supervisor. He seems pretty confident, so I guess it's all right."

Joe tells Bill that the checklist is complete but once again he expresses concern about the temperature.

"Look, if it makes you feel any better, I'll go ahead and initial the checklist. That way I take responsibility. But I'm positive that there isn't a problem, so let's just get the show on the road." Bill takes the sheet and signs his name on the dotted line.

Joe gives it one last try. "Bill, it wouldn't take Instruments & Controls a minute to check it out, just to be safe. Besides …"

"That's enough, Joe. Just shut up!" replies Bill, cutting Joe off. "I said it's okay and it is, so let's get this place started up."

The startup continues as scheduled. A review taken at a later time reveals that the auxiliary feedwater discharge temperature was extraordinarily high, causing the auxiliary feed pump to be declared inoperable, resulting in a federal violation by the plant.

This authoritarian orientation to problem solving is obviously self-defeating. The necessary data from others, the evaluation of their inputs, and the testing of hypotheses are critical to success. The authoritarian leadership style has the effect of shutting out the input that others can contribute and therefore jeopardizing success Bill is convinced he is right and is more interested in pushing his point of view than listening to Joe. He is determined to accomplish the startup on his shift and ignores the need to correct the auxiliary feed pump discharge temperature.

Here is another example:

Shift A is standing their first day of the mid-shift (0000–0800). The plant is in a normal configuration for 50 percent reactor power. Preparations have been made to increase power to 80 percent.

The shift supervisor, John, gives the order to commence the power increase. Earl, the reactor operator, commences rod withdrawal to increase power. As reactor power approaches 60 percent, Earl calls Jim, the control room operator (CRO), over to his panel. "Channel 1 power indication appears to be high by about 5 percent," Earl states.

"That channel always indicates a little high at this power level," Jim replies.

Earl isn't satisfied with Jim's dismissal of the situation. As Karl, the shift technical advisor (STA), comes by to check the rod pattern, Earl states his concern to him. Karl agrees with Earl, "Channel 1 usually indicates higher than the others but not by this much." While Karl and Earl continue their discussion, Jim speaks with John concerning the indication difference, and John agrees that no problem exists.

John sees that Earl and Karl are having a discussion. As he approaches the control panel, he discovers that Earl has not been increasing reactor power as expected. John asks, "Why aren't we raising reactor power? We should be at 70 percent by now." Earl replies by explaining that a 5 percent indication difference exists between Channel 1 and the remaining channels. John states in a brittle tone, "Jim has already discussed that with me, and I agree with him. This is nothing unusual, and I've already decided what we're going to do."

Earl tries to object, "It just seems to Karl and me that the indication is higher than normal."

"And it seems to me," says John, "that we have all wasted as much time on this as we're going to. Now start increasing power."

John doesn't like anyone stepping on his turf. He feels threatened when another operator sees a problem. After all, he *knows* his stuff. Therefore he cuts off information and suppresses disagreement in order to win his position. Earl will do as he is told, but he will most likely resent it. And the next time a similar situation arises, he may be reluctant to voice his opinion.

Conventional wisdom has been extrapolated from less complicated operations for use in more complex situations; however, this approach is incorrect. New leadership skills need to be acquired to allow the shift supervisor to be more open to input from others. Solutions to complicated operational problems require reliance on deriving, cross-referencing, and synthesizing data from multiple sources; working through discrepancies; and dealing with contradictions. This approach permits the gathering of information from many operators with possible solutions to be analyzed for validity prior to being implemented.

By tapping all control room resources, the shift supervisor approaches the solution to the problem in a way that should produce a more orderly approach. This increases the likelihood of identifying valid options and results in more effective solutions.

When shift supervisors are more open to input from others, they are not weaker and subject to insubordination. This openness is in terms of input; who decides or what decision is made still remains with the shift supervisor. When no one is in charge, decisiveness is lost and chaos is the likely result. This is not the case in a teamwork situation.

These illustrations demonstrate the problem of ineffectively exercising power and authority. This problem extends far beyond the cockpit, the surgical amphitheater, or the nuclear plant floor—often right up to the boardroom itself.

Charles W. Parry, CEO and Alcoa man to the core, was seen to be the "problem" preventing the company from moving forward. Board members deliberated on this matter. They determined it was in the best interest of the company to remove this "obstacle" to progress, asking Parry to step down from his post. What was Parry's reaction? It caught him completely by surprise, causing him to feel they should have given him some indication of their displeasure. Says Parry, "They never did." Furthermore, the next man in line for succession was bypassed, indicating that the problem was seen to be more pervasive than Parry alone. For the first time in Alcoa's 99-year history, a successor was brought in from the outside. This total break from the past sent shock waves through the Alcoa culture, "surprising the living daylights" out of tradition-bound Alcoa executives. Our point in mentioning Parry is that it portrays yet another example of poor team process within a stagnant organization culture; those immersed in it seem unable to see the forest for the trees.[22]

General Motors (GM) has experienced a significant loss of market share in recent times and, although the years of downtrend have been arrested, efforts to recoup market share have not been productive. The reasons for this poor performance may lie once again in a deteriorating organization culture. Over the years, the organization had become fixed, unchanging, and unresponsive—even resistant—to new and emerging trends. Elmer Johnson at age 56 has now left his post as executive vice president. His departure, one step away from the chairmanship, has made him the second internal critic to leave the company's top ranks in several years. The first was H. Ross Perot, who had come in from the outside related to the Electronic Data Systems (EDS) buy-out. Roger Smith, the powerful chairman of GM, lost his enchantment with both gentlemen. Each was eliminated as their push for change became too extreme—and too threatening—for GM's change-resistant culture. In fact, Perot had taken on the role of internal—as well as public—critic, something GM's staid bureaucracy was unable and unwilling to tolerate. By analogy, GM rejected such behavior as an immune system resists an infection.[23]

Merrill Lynch provides a third corporate illustration. A major financial services concern, it sought entrenchment in the London financial markets. Britain's top bond trader, John Hutchinson, was brought on board to lead the assault. After assembling a top-notch team, steps were taken to get new business by cutting margins and absorbing losses. These efforts were apparently successful as market share increased by 20 percent. However, the scene soon changed to one of shrinking operations with market share dropping to an unattractive 4 percent. Obviously, Hutchinson was out, but what was the reason for his failure? The overriding problem was management, that is, the top movers at Merrill lacked a cohesive way of thinking and working together. The golden-haired boys brought in by Hutchinson separated off into fiefdoms, and the result was internal competition and fighting over bonuses, resources, and credit for accounts. Everyone was operating at odds, rather than seeking synergistic collaboration in a teamwork sense that could move them toward common objectives.[24]

What is the common thread running through each of these illustrations? An aluminum manufacturer, the world's giant automobile producer, and financial institutions such as Merrill Lynch might at one level seem quite dissimilar. The technologies are different, the qualifications of technical and managerial personnel are not comparable, the customers with whom they deal are distinctly unique; yet we find the same core problem characterizes them all. All are giant companies; the common theme is teamwork at the top—or the lack of it. These three are just the tip of the iceberg—the underlying dynamics run deep within organizations, across, and up and down all levels. The real cause of the tragedy portrayed in each example is occasioned by poor, or nonexistent, teamwork within a broader culture that fails to support sound human interaction.

References

1. Blake, R. R., and J. S. Mouton. 1985. *The Managerial Grid III.* Houston: Gulf Publishing, p. 12.

2. Englade, K. F. 1988. "Better Managers in the Friendly Skies." *Across the Board*, June, 36–45.

3. Cockpit Resource Management Seminar materials. Copyright © 1983, Scientific Methods, Inc.

4. National Transportation Safety Board, *Safety Recommendation(s) A-85-26 and -27*, Washington, D.C. (Issued April 15, 1985), pp. 1–5.

5. Blake, R. R., J. S. Mouton (Scientific Methods, Inc.), and

Command/Leadership/ Resource Management Steering Committee and Working Groups (United Airlines). 1982. *Cockpit Resource Management.* Denver/Austin: Cockpit Resource Management.

6. Pantin, H. M., and C. S. Carver. 1982. "Induced Competence and the Bystander Effect." *Journal of Applied Social Psychology,* 12, No. 2, 110–11.

7. Lantane, B., and J. M. Darley. 1968. "Group Inhibition of Bystander Intervention in Emergencies." *Journal of Personality and Social Psychology,* 10, No. 3, 215–21.

8. *Ibid.*

9. Langer, F. J., and A. Benevento. 1978. "Self-Induced Dependence." *Journal of Personality and Social Psychology,* 36, No. 8, 886–93.

10. Baumeister, R. F., S. P. Chesner, P. S. Senders, and D. M. Tice. 1988. "Who's in Charge Here? Group Leaders Do Lend Help in Emergencies." *Personality and Social Psychology Bulletin,* 14, No. 1, 17–22.

11. Hamblin, R. L. 1958. "Leadership and Crises." *Sociometry,* 21, 322–35.

12. Langer and Benevento, *op cit.*

13. Hamblin, *op cit.*

14. Hamblin, *op cit.*

15. Blake, R. R., and J. S. Mouton. 1964. *The Managerial Grid.* Houston: Gulf Publishing.

16. Blake, R. R., J. S. Mouton, L. B. Barnes, and L.E. Greiner. 1964. "Breakthrough in Organization Development." *Harvard Business Review,* 42, No. 6, 133–55.

17. Blake, R. R., and J. S. Mouton. 1986. *Executive Achievement: Making It at the Top.* New York: McGraw-Hill.

18. Blake, R. R., and J. S. Mouton. 1987. *GridWorks.* Austin: Scientific Methods.

19. Blake, R. R., J. S. Mouton, and M. S. Williams. 1981. *The Academic Administrator Grid.* San Francisco: Jossey-Bass.

20. Prather, S. E., R. R. Blake, and J. S. Mouton. 1988. *Caring for Difficult Patients: Beyond Medical Excellence through Physician Leadership.* Austin: Scientific Methods, Inc., 124–125.

21. Blake, R. R., in collaboration with Special Task Force from Scientific Methods, Inc., and Institute of Nuclear Power Opera-

tions. 1988. *Control Room Resource Management.* Austin: Scientific Methods.

22. Burrough, B., and C. Hymowitz. "Alcoa's Chief Parry Says His Retirement Was Sought By Outside Board Members." *The Wall Street Journal,* April 24, 1987, 39.

23. Lee, A. 1988. *Call Me Roger.* Chicago: Contemporary Books, p. 198; Ingrassia, P., and J. M. Schlesinger. "GM Announces Big Shake-Up of Executives." *The Wall Street Journal,* June 28, 1988, 2.

24. Forman, C. "Merrill Scales Down London Ambitions." *The Wall Street Journal,* June 15, 1988, 16.

2

The Grid

In this chapter, by going a step beyond the cockpit into general management, we take a broader view in order to illustrate the utility of Grid as a general management tool for conceptual analysis of how behavior impedes or promotes successful outcomes. The interest of organization development centers on profit and nonprofit organizations alike—business and commercial corporations; service institutions; colleges, schools, and universities; the medical arena and hospitals. We have found the list to be endless.

The Managerial Grid

The Managerial Grid clarifies and crystallizes many of the fundamentals of behavior dynamics in business. Any individual who is working for a firm has assigned responsibilities. This is true whether the person works at a very low level or high up in the organization. If this person is a manager, there are two primary concerns. One is concern for production—the results of his or her efforts. This is indicated by the horizontal axis on the Grid. The manager's degree of concern is indicated on a nine-point continuum where 9 denotes a high degree of concern and 1 shows a low degree of concern. The second concern is for people—subordinates, colleagues, or higher level bosses. The vertical axis represents the manager's concern for people, with the degree of concern depicted on a nine-point scale with 9 being high concern and 1 being low concern. These two axes show us how the two concerns interact and come together to create a single coherent attitude in the case of each Grid style.

Each of these attitudes, or Grid styles, describes different ways in which managers think about accomplishing results with and through people. These same Grid styles also describe patterns of interaction among managers within an organization that constitute corporate culture. The manner in which these two concerns integrate into one attitude that is expressed in a person's behavior defines how authority is used. For example, when high concern for people is coupled with a low concern for production, the leader wants people to be friendly and happy. This is far different than the leader characterized by a high concern for people and a high concern for production. In the second case, the leader wants people to be involved and committed to the work and to strive enthusiastically to make problem-solving contributions to organizational success.

Although these two concerns can be united in numerous ways, only a few are important for understanding the exercise of leadership and the culture that develops as a result. Each of these theories or orientations rests on a different set of assumptions for using power and authority to link people into production. An orientation is a way of thinking about or analyzing a problem that is subject to change to another orientation as a result of increased understanding. Thus an orientation is not a fixed or unchanging trait.

The important point is that to increase the managerial competence and the productivity of people, a leader must know of alternative leadership styles and be prepared to select and act upon the soundest one. From the range of orientations, six display such significant differences in characteristic actions and outcomes that they are readily identified as benchmark styles. These include 9,9; 9,1; 1,9; Paternalism; 5,5; and 1,1. In this sequence we will look at the six styles and provide illustrations to show how they might operate in a real-life situation.

Since the Grid has already been shown in a specialized form for the cockpit in Chapter 1, we will not repeat it here. You may, however, wish to refer to Fig. 1–1 to see it once again in its "big picture" formulation. As we "go around the Grid" describing the different attitudes managers may embrace we will "zoom in" on the section of the Grid being discussed.

To be useful, the illustration we provide for each Grid style needs to be within the experience of most readers. The receptionist coming into her or his first job might be a good point to begin. Almost everyone can identify with a new receptionist trying to learn the ropes since most of us have had the common experience of first employment. Therefore, substitute yourself for this new individual coming onto the corporate scene and see if you recall any of the bosses depicted in the illustrations. This may help to clarify the different Grid styles as you are reminded of the approach you encountered in your first job.

Although your initial position may have varied across a broad range—a manual job; a military role; a young executive, perhaps with an M.B.A or Ph.D.; a high tech specialist—the receptionist example can be useful in helping you reconstruct these early events in your work career. Furthermore, it can shed light on your relationships today, whether with bosses, colleagues, or subordinates.

We start with the 9,9 approach, which integrates the people and production concerns at a high level. Then we portray other Grid styles in shorter vignettes of the same situation in order to provide you with a basis for comparison.

The 9,9 Approach

In the upper right corner of the Grid is the 9,9 orientation (Fig. 2–1). The individual oriented in this way stresses fact finding as the key to problem resolution. The 9,9-oriented manager seeks input from others and creates a forum for open and candid discussion, confronting disagreement in such a way as to air doubts and

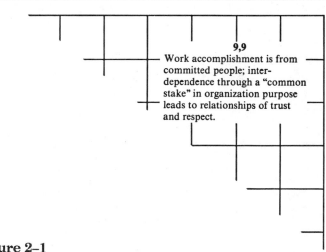

Figure 2–1
9,9: Team Management

reservations in order to achieve mutual understanding and full commitment to the conclusions reached. The 9,9 theory is synergistic—people working together have a common stake in the outcome of their endeavors and therefore mesh their effort interdependently.

The following example illustrates the 9,9 approach. It is based on a simple scene between a boss and a new receptionist in a company called Strategic Systems, Inc., and it involves a discussion of the receptionist's job responsibilities.

Boss: This is your first day. It's likely to be a little tough. How do you feel?

Receptionist: I'm all thumbs. I don't know what to do.

Boss: Then that's a good place to begin. That's where we start setting goals. What is your understanding of this job?

Receptionist: Well, I'm to be the receptionist. I've never had any experience with that.

Boss: Let's look at what a receptionist does.

Receptionist: Well, one thing you do is answer the phone.

Boss: Yes, what else?

Receptionist: Greet visitors, type some.

Boss: Anything else?

Receptionist: I'd be expected to be your person Friday.

Boss: Maybe. That's a good overview of the whole job. Let's talk about those things, one at a time. Telephone answering is our first contact with our clients. Let's talk about goals for answering the phone.

Receptionist: What goals? What's that got to do with answering the telephone?

Boss: Let me ask you a question. How do you feel when the phone rings twenty times and there is no answer?

Receptionist: I don't like it. Either no one is there or people are too busy, or they are visiting ...

Boss: I don't like to be kept waiting either. Can we set an objective for prompt answering?

Receptionist: Maybe I can answer it within the first several rings. I can experiment with it to see if I can get it down to three.

Boss: That sounds fine. Now, what's the best thing to say?

Receptionist: "Good morning."

Boss: But then the caller doesn't know whether it's the right number.

Receptionist: I could say, "Good morning. This is Strategic Systems, Inc."

Boss: That's it ... what we've talked about so far covers a lot of detail, but it shows that goals are involved in just answering the phone.

Receptionist: Yes it does ... but, I'll never remember it all.

Boss: It'll take a little practice. I'll go to a phone and call as though I were a real caller. We can critique how the call went after you deal with me.

Receptionist: That's a good idea. That way I can check myself out.

The boss goes about getting involvement by sharing empathic feelings with the receptionist at the very beginning. From then on the discussion is problem focused and learning centered, aiding the new employee to think through the situation in a proactive way and to explore with the boss how the situation is seen. In this manner the boss quickly learns "where the receptionist is coming from." This enables the boss to formulate subsequent questions in terms that are immediately meaningful. The receptionist's overview indicates comprehension of the job requirements even though the work had not previously been done. From there on out the discussion builds to a joint plan of action. The receptionist can be expected to own the goals that emerged and therefore to be committed to achieving them.

The 9,1 Approach

In the lower right corner of the Grid, 9,1 (Fig. 2–2) represents high concern for results but little for the people who are expected to implement the work.

The following example portrays a 9,1-oriented boss interacting with a new receptionist. Notice how it differs from a 9,9-oriented way of handling the same situation.

Boss: This is your first day. I want you to get off to a good start, so I'll tell you exactly what I want, when I want it, and how I want it done. That way, there should be no mistakes.

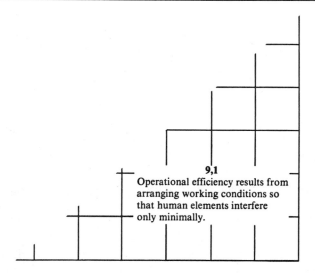

9,1
Operational efficiency results from arranging working conditions so that human elements interfere only minimally.

Figure 2–2
9,1: Authority-Obedience

Receptionist: May I ask questions?

Boss: I don't think you'll need to. I'll be very clear and specific about what you are to do.

Receptionist: What about "Why?"

Boss: About your asking questions—no need. I'll tell you what you need to know. Perhaps you can ask questions later. We'll see.

Receptionist: But, what if ...

Boss: Your job is to be my receptionist. Your goals are to answer the phone, greet visitors, type, and be my person Friday.

Receptionist: That sounds okay.

Boss: First, about answering the phone. I don't like to have a caller wait. Therefore, I expect you to answer every call within three rings. And I want you to say, "Good morning. This is Strategic Systems, Inc. May I be of help?" Do you understand?

Receptionist: I think so.

(Phone rings.)

Boss: Pick it up.

Receptionist: Hello, oh, I mean, this is Strategic Systems, Inc. What did you want? Oh, wait a minute.

(Transfers phone call.)

Boss: Look, I'll spell it out for you one more time. Now ...

This is a 9,1-oriented approach because the boss imposes demands on the receptionist, while denying the subordinate any opportunity to contribute to the outcome. The imposed goals may be crystal clear, but the receptionist feels no sense of ownership. Furthermore, if the goals appear impossible to achieve, thinly disguised emotions of resentment lead to negative reactions intended to show the boss "why it can't be done." Thus the two possible outcomes to a 9,1 approach are suppression/compliance or fighting.

The 1,9 Approach

At the opposite corner of the Grid, in the top left, the 1,9 theory (Fig. 2–3) puts major emphasis on people and little on the results required to sustain an ongoing business.

The previous approach, 9,1, concentrated on results. In contrast, the 1,9-oriented manager is concerned with maintaining harmonious relationships with people, placing results second. As you read the following example, notice how it differs from the first two styles that were presented, particularly contrasting the "9" of 1,9 (people), and the "9" of 9,1 (results) with the integrated 9's in the 9,9 approach.

Boss: This is your first day. I want you to be happy here.

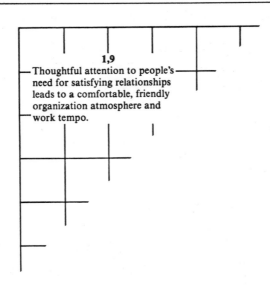

Figure 2–3
1,9: Country Club Management

Receptionist: Gee, I'm all thumbs. I don't know what to do.

Boss: Don't worry. Everybody feels like that when they first get started. I want you to feel at home and to do the job in a way that feels natural to you. How does that sound?

Receptionist: Oh, I like that very much. You know, no two people are exactly the same.

Boss: You're absolutely right. Tell me how you would like to get started.

Receptionist: Well, I hate to cause any inconvenience, but I would really like my desk over here. I like looking out the window.

Boss: It is a beautiful view. I'll arrange for maintenance to come and do that for you.

(Phone rings.)

Boss: Oh, please pick it up.

Receptionist: Hello? Yes, this is Strategic Systems, Inc. Well, I don't know. Wait a minute. (turns to boss) They want Joe Turner. Is he here?

Boss: Oh, yes, he should be in the next office. Let me run over and see. I'll be right back.

This 1,9 approach stimulates the receptionist to think and speak in an open and spontaneous way. That's all fine and good, but, as can be seen in the example, it leads to self-centeredness—"move my desk over here," "I like looking out the window." The receptionist undoubtedly feels right at home, but goals of running a businesslike office are sacrificed in the process.

The 1,9–9,1 Approach: Paternalism

Paternalism is to some extent a blending of the 9,1 and 1,9 theories (Fig. 2–4). This approach couples the concern for controlling people in a 9,1 way with the loving and helpful attender of 1,9. The

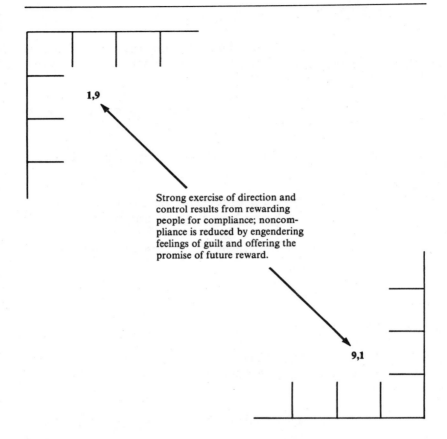

Figure 2–4
9,1–1,9: Paternalism

basic assumption of the boss toward a subordinate is, "I own (or am responsible for) you and want to help your career (much as if the other person were a son or daughter). That's why I expect your loyalty as a matter of course." Benevolent autocrat is another name for the paternalist.

In the following example of the paternalistic approach, notice the aspects of 1,9 and 9,1 that are incorporated within it.

Boss: This is your first day. I want you to get off to a good start, so let's talk about what you are supposed to do. Now, I'll go slowly so you can understand. Your job is to answer the phone, greet visitors, and do a little typing. And, of course, once in a while I may ask you to do a few personal errands for me. Sound easy enough?

Receptionist: Well, it sounds like a lot. I'll be lucky if I can get the phone right.

Boss: Oh, it's really nothing at all. I'm sure a smart individual like you won't have any difficulty accomplishing these small tasks. Now, let me continue. About the phone, I want it answered within three rings. And I want you to say, "Good morning. This is Mr. Jones' office. May I be of help?"

Receptionist: What if I get two calls, or what if a visitor walks in at the same time as the phone rings?

Boss: That's a good question and I'll be happy to explain. I'm sure you would want to give priority to the first one. That means that if the phone rings first, the caller gets priority. Or, if the visitor arrives first, the visitor gets priority. Do you understand?

Receptionist: Well, I think so.

Boss: Well, let me explain. If you're on the phone, tell the caller, "One moment, please. A visitor has just walked in." Then tell the visitor to have a seat and say, "I'll be with you as soon as possible." Then return to the caller and finish that business. Alternatively, do the same if you're talking with a visitor and the phone rings.

Receptionist: Oh, I'm getting confused. You know, I hate to keep people waiting.

Boss: Well, that's the test of a good receptionist. I am confident that you can do it.

(Phone rings.)

Receptionist: Hello. Oh, I mean, Good morning. Can I help you? Oh, this is Mr. Jones' office. Oh, okay.

(Transfers call.)

Boss: Whoops. You slipped up! Remember, "Good morning. This is Mr. Jones' office. Can I be of help?" Okay?

Receptionist: Oh, dear, I'm not sure.

Boss: Well, I'm going to help you. I'll be calling in from my other line today, anonymously, of course, and that way you can get some practice. Then we'll *both* see how well you can do.

This paternalistic boss is thoughtful of the receptionist's feelings and wants to stimulate a positive attitude. Using compliments to induce cooperation is one way: "a smart individual like you," or "that's a good question." The boss also wants to make the job look easy: "these small tasks," "it's really nothing at all." All of these seek to induce compliance on the receptionist's part while trying to conceal the tight control that is really being imposed.

The positive side of all this is that the boss can expect to receive the desired result, i.e., the receptionist will do it in the required way. The negative side is that the receptionist is likely to become dependent. A person who knows how to listen and accept directions is unlikely to exercise initiative in behalf of the office, waiting instead to be told what to do.

The 5,5 Approach

In the center of the Grid is the 5,5 style (Fig. 2–5). The idea is, "Get results, but don't kill yourself. Do the job but find a comfortable tempo. Don't push too hard or others will think you are pushy. At the same time, don't let people off too easily or you will be seen as soft. Be fair but firm."

The following example portrays the 5,5 Grid style. It seeks to achieve a balance between production and people.

Boss: Hi, I'm Bill Smith. You must be Sue. We've been expecting you.

Receptionist: Oh, hello, Mr. Smith. Yes, I'm Susan Turner. Reporting for duty.

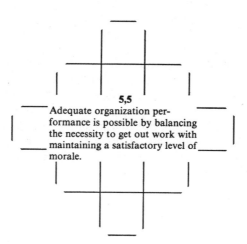

5,5
Adequate organization performance is possible by balancing
the necessity to get out work with
maintaining a satisfactory level of
morale.

Figure 2–5
5,5: Organization Man Management

Boss: Ha, ha. I like that. You've got a sense of humor. By the way, we're real informal around here. Just call be Bill. Now, let me fill you in about the office. We're known as the "PMA Bunch"—that's Positive Mental Attitude. Think you'll fit in?

Receptionist: Well, gee, I hope so. I'll certainly try.

Boss: Yes, we're one big happy family. Makes the work enjoyable, you know. There's always lots to be done, but the point is we do it together. Now, your job is to answer the phone plus one or two other things, but I'll let you know as we get there. Making a good impression, conveying that feeling of enthusiasm, is all important. We're known for that, you know. We don't want to lose it.

Receptionist: Yes, I understand.

Boss: It's in your smile; it's in your walk; it's in your talk—well, everything.

Receptionist: It all sounds very nice.

Boss: Oh, but it's much more than nice. It gets the job done—in a good way. I can already see that you're one of us. Glad to have you aboard, mate!

The 5,5-oriented boss recognizes the need to get results, but this is balanced with a need to keep people happy. Unlike the 9,9 approach, an integration is not seen as a possibility, so the boss seeks a happy medium. The new receptionist is welcomed into the fold and made to feel right at home, but at the same time it is made clear, albeit superficially, that the work is important as well. "Good enough" or maximizing the status quo seems to be a good credo for 5,5.

The 1,1 Approach

In the lower left Grid corner is 1,1 (Fig. 2–6). In this case, the manager has little concern for either people or production, simply going through the motions of being part of the firm without really contributing to its purpose. The 1,1-oriented manager has not actually quit the job but he or she has walked out mentally, perhaps many years before. Such managers are freeloaders, creating a drag on organizational effectiveness in the here-and-now.

Look at the following example and see if you can recognize the 1,1 Grid style.

Boss: Yes? Are you looking for someone?

Receptionist: I'm the new receptionist. Are you Mr. Smith?

Boss: Well, yes, but I don't know anything about this. Oh, wait a minute. Seems like I got a memo ...

Receptionist: Well, they told me to report to you for an orientation.

Boss: They did, huh? Well, it's all pretty cut and dried. I guess that's your desk, your phone, your file cabinet. Any questions?

Receptionist: This is my first job. It would help if you would walk me through what I'm supposed to do.

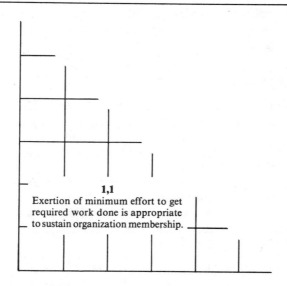

1,1
Exertion of minimum effort to get required work done is appropriate to sustain organization membership.

Figure 2–6
1,1: Impoverished Management

Boss: Oh, one of the other girls can do that. They know the score. Just grab one and ask her.

(Phone rings.)

Receptionist: Should I answer it?

Boss: No, it's still five to eight. We don't officially open until eight. But that reminds me. When I get a call, never say that I'm here. Always take a message. That's the way I like it.

Receptionist: Well, okay. I'm really not sure what I'm doing.

Boss: Well, I wouldn't worry about it. I'm sure you'll catch on. We all do.

This boss is barely there. As far as the new receptionist is concerned, he might as well be miles away. Little help has been provided either in terms of understanding the work to be done or in aiding the new employee to feel comfortable about the job. The attitude is, "I don't care."

Grid Style Elements

As can be seen in the examples just illustrated, the exercise of leadership can take many forms. Some approaches are clearly more effective than others. Leadership is a complex process, but we can gain a deeper understanding of managerial style by identifying key elements. Although these elements may be examined in isolation, it is useful to think of them as different facets of the same thing, that is, they fit together to make a whole.

The elements we use in describing Grid style are initiative, inquiry, advocacy, conflict resolution, decision making, and critique. A brief synopsis of each follows:

1. *Initiative*—Initiative is exercised whenever effort is concentrated on a specific activity to start something that was not going on before, to stop something that was occurring, or to shift direction and character of effort. A leader may take initiative or avoid taking initiative even when others expect action.

2. *Inquiry*—Inquiry permits a leader to gain access to facts and data. The quality of inquiry may depend on a leader's thoroughness. A leader may have very low personal standards of thoroughness and thus ignore the need for inquiry. Alternatively, standards may be high and every attempt made to learn as much as possible about work activities.

3. *Advocacy*—To advocate is to take a position. A leader may have strong convictions but think it risky to take a stand. On the other hand, a leader may have low or nonexistent convictions and therefore be inclined not to state a point of view. In other cases, a leader may embrace a position simply to oppose another person in an effort to "win," pursuing a goal of "Who's right," not "What's right."

4. *Conflict Resolution*—When people have different ideas and express them, conflict is inevitable. Although conflict can be destructive and disruptive, it also can be constructive and creative. It all depends on how it is handled. A

leader who faces up to conflict with others, resolving it in a way that leads to mutual understanding, evokes confidence and respect. The inability to cope with conflict effectively leads to lack of trust and confidence and may result in feelings of hostility, frustration, and despair.

5. *Decision Making*—Decision making is the key that permits leadership to be applied to performance. This may involve solo decision making, in which the leader acts alone as ultimate decision maker. Alternatively, it may mean delegation of responsibilities for decisions, as is true of 9,9 teamwork. In this case, all available resources are brought to bear on making and implementing decisions.

6. *Critique*—Critique describes a variety of useful ways to study and solve operational problems that members face either singly or collectively as they seek to carry out their assignments. It is a process of stepping away from or interrupting an activity to study it, to see alternative possibilities for improving performance, and to anticipate and avoid any activities that may have adverse consequences.

Are All Elements Equal?

The boss/receptionist illustrations provide useful examples for how these elements of leadership are exercised in the various Grid styles. The question might be asked, "Are all these elements of equal importance?" No, we believe one is key to gaining access to all the others. This one is critique. When managers become willing and ready to engage in critique and to take it seriously, strengths and weaknesses in people's behavior become available to public and individual examination. Critique is a tool of change critical to sound management.

Critique can be used to:

1. Gain insight into your own theory of management by learning how others experience your exercise of power and authority.

2. Listen to yourself talk, learning to observe how you conduct yourself on the phone, in management meetings, with coworkers and subordinates, and so on. In other words, you discover the common thread that runs

throughout your interactions with people, and thus you gain an objective view of your own management style.

3. Examine consequences of the actions you take. That is, it enables you to look at the end result and to ask, "What did *I* do to bring this about?" and "What could *I* do differently to achieve a better or more desirable result?"

For example, think about how your team operates. First, ask yourself, "How has it worked in the past?" Compare this to the consequences, or results achieved, from the modes of interaction used by the team. Now your team is in a position to ask itself, "What can we do to make ourselves more effective? How can each person change or modify behavior to become a stronger contributor to the team effort?"

Critique offers organization members a way in which to influence outcomes and therefore a way in which to move beyond the status quo and to fulfill a vision of tomorrow. It is a step that is often bypassed or overlooked despite its important role in bringing about real and enduring change. However, when used, critique permits a top team constantly to rethink the shape of a corporation, comparing what history—tradition, precedent, and past practice—has dictated versus throwing off the shackles of the past and challenging organization membership to achieve greatness.

In summary, critique offers an opportunity for change, growth, and development. It can unlock mysteries, reveal hidden assets, anticipate barriers to success, define corporate vision, and stimulate the imagination. Its uses are endless. This is why the element of critique is central, and other management tools wane by comparison.

Summary

The six Grid styles outlined in this chapter are each based on a set of assumptions about how to achieve production with and through people. These assumptions may or may not be sound. In either case, however, sound or unsound, assumptions become part and parcel of a person's basic beliefs. They serve to guide behavior and therefore constitute a manager's Grid style.

If our assumptions are unsound, the question is, of course, "How can they be changed?" Obviously, a first step is to become aware of the assumptions on which we act. The Grid helps us do this.

Once we become aware of the depth and character of our assumptions, we are then in a position to analyze them in order to gain an understanding of the positive and negative consequences of our actions. Until people are able to see this direct correlation between assumptions, behavior, and consequences, change remains a remote possibility.

The single most significant premise on which Grid Organization Development rests is that managers universally acknowledge that the 9,9 way of solving problems is the soundest way to achieve excellence. This conclusion has been verified through empirical statistical studies around the world.[1] The 9,9 theory defines a model that people, based on their own convictions, say they want, not only as a model for their own conduct, but also as a model for what they want their companies to become.

We examine the first step in this process in the Managerial Grid Seminar, presented in Chapter 5. First, however, we turn our attention to the big picture—organization culture—in Chapter 3. Then we take a look at strategies for diagnosing this culture to assess real needs in Chapter 4.

Reference

1. Blake, R. R., and J. S. Mouton. 1968. *Corporate Excellence Through Grid Organization Development*. Houston: Gulf Publishing, p. 63.

3

Corporate Culture and Commitment to Change

In the cockpit change project described in Chapter 1, captains found the learning experience of having to lead an open problem-solving cockpit to be of fundamental value. Thereafter they recommitted themselves from a ten o'clock (9,1) to a two o'clock (9,9) point of view as the soundest and safest way to operate. However, upon returning to the flight line, they met with frustration. First and second officers did not respond, and eventually the captains returned to the ten o'clock way of leading. What they had done again demonstrates the fadeout phenomenon to which we have already alluded. But this is not the end of the story. The question to be answered is, "Why did this happen?"

The answer lies in culture. Change requires all norms-carriers from the ten o'clock culture, that is, captains, first officers, and second officers, to participate in the same commitment to change. This gives all members a common or shared framework within which to think about, discuss, and practice the fullest possible mobilization of human resources for performing effectively within the cockpit operational system. What has been said thus far has been in the context of the cockpit, but it is equally applicable in seeking culture change in other operational systems.

How to Recognize Corporate Culture

Culture can be recognized by examining the attitudes, beliefs, and opinions that people communicate to one another on a day-in and day-out basis. Culture includes the traditions, precedents, and long-established practices that have become customs for interrelating and solving problems. These are the rules and guidelines that tell members how to participate, what to do, and what not to do. The following example shows how team culture affects work relationships.

Cindy Washington and Sam Blanks are department managers. The division in which they work is responsible for operations as well as marketing, sales, distribution, financial control, and overall profit and loss.

Cindy and Sam have just come from a meeting of the manager and key department heads in which Cindy submitted a new and unprecedented proposal.

Cindy: Sam, I'm leaving the company.

Sam: You're kidding, Cindy.

Cindy: No, I've had it. I don't know where I'm going to go, but I've had it up to here with this running dogfight.

Sam: Dogfight?

Cindy: Sure, you saw what it was like today.

Sam: Just like any other day as far as I can see.

Cindy: Yeah, and that's just what I mean. But today was a special case for me. I worked night and day on that proposal, and you saw how it went. It's the whole atmosphere. And there doesn't seem to be any hope. I like a good argument, but what we're doing is not productive. It takes a lot longer to push something through than it does to develop it. And even when it's done, the end result is a watered-down version of a good solution. Look at today and tell me—honestly—if it was any different than last week, or the week before, or the week before that.

Sam: Well, you've got a point there.

Cindy: Yeah, in the end, we just blew two hours in frustration—a bunch of kids trying to get their own way. I've got better things to do. Look at my notepad. I measure the quality of the day by the absence of doodles—there isn't a place left to scrawl. In the end, Will, our fair-haired friend from finance, took the big lead. The others were too tired of fighting. And what was the result? No real answer. There wasn't a grain of substance left in the decision we reached. It stank. And all because no one wanted to give in.

Cindy is discussing corporate culture. One thing is certain, Cindy is not happy with her membership in the organization. As a matter of fact, she's so unhappy, she wants to leave. The source of her displeasure is the character of participation. But when Cindy's situation is viewed in another way, what is really going on?

Two very fundamental issues are involved in Cindy's dilemma. One is power and authority, how conflict is dealt with, and what it does to everyone's participation. The other is the uniformity of response, that is, the prevailing norms that determine how organization members interact with one another. These two fundamental issues of organizational psychology are at the very heart of the matter of participation.

We recognize that almost universal agreement exists that increased participation is the key for solving problems of productivity, quality, creativity, satisfaction, and so on. Why not simply put it on the line and let everybody know that they should work for increased participation, that it is expected of them, and that they will be rewarded in accordance with how much of it they get?

That seems to be where difficulties begin. It is one thing to want participation and quite another to create the conditions under which effective participation takes place. Something more is required than an edict, pronouncement, or promise of reward. This leads to the question, "What barriers have to be removed to achieve the desired degree of participation?"

There seem to be two preconditions for this:

1. How authority is exercised. Remember, as shown in Chapter 2, some ways of exercising authority stifle or kill participation and others release it. Some permit it but the quality is low.

2. Pressures to conform. Informal norms by which people regulate their interactions may be adverse to effective participation. Members are more likely to conform to what is expected of them rather than suffer the risk of being seen as troublemakers, nonadapters, or intrac-

tables exercising so much independence as to be out of control.

Any approach to elicit stronger and more effective participation must deal with these two factors.

Let's go back to Cindy and Sam. Cindy said the meeting was ineffective because no one wanted to give in. As they continue to talk, Sam responds to Cindy's statement.

Sam: Well, this is serious, Cindy. I think we should talk this through a bit. I know we had a pretty heavy session, but isn't that the price of excellence? You know Alan pushes every subject.

Cindy: That's just the point. The push has nothing to do with excellence. The whole company is full of counterpunchers.

Sam: You're probably the brightest systems person in the company. We've got to get to the bottom of this. You can't just sulk and quit. We need you—especially now. What's really troubling you? Why do you call us "counterpunchers"?

Cindy: Take John, for example. He's so afraid of failure that he nitpicks a proposal to death. He misses the thrust and digs at little trivialities that don't matter a bit. It's not perfectionism; it's raw fear. He's terrified at the thought of agreement and action.

Sam: I see what you're driving at.

Cindy: And Bob. He's numero uno in his own mind. He's got to run everything. He is so concerned with keeping things his own way that he just can't let another person take the lead.

Sam: Score two for the sage; I never thought about it like that.

Cindy: You saw what happened today. It was cutthroat and counterpunch all the way. Not only with me. Alan twisted your idea until it fit his own. And remember the scene between Bob and George. Red faces. Table thumping. It was a real standoff.

Sam: You're right. I can't deny it.

Cindy: And then it became a free for all. We spent over two hours on the subject. The rest of us tried to break it up, but resolution was impossible. So what did we end up with? A straw of an idea—a little bit of George, a little of Bob, a little of the boss—to break the impasse. Honestly now, do you think that will fly? No one has any commitment to it. It was just an escape from three guys slashing away at each other. Mark my words. That plan will either go belly up at the next meeting or else it will die in the implementation.

Sam: Well, I know Alan tries to manage conflict by calling a halt to arguments. Otherwise, I think he lets us go at it a bit rather than being the one to declare a winner.

Cindy: Well, when things reach an impasse, Alan calls the shots. I'll agree that he lets people give a rationale, and I admire him for that.

Sam: At least it's better than last year when he dealt with everyone individually.

Cindy: Yeah. That almost brought us to a halt. Each of us was doing our own thing and none of it fit together. Talk about chaos!

Sam: I remember. We sure got hung up ... Do you think we should avoid conflict?

Cindy: Sam, you know as well as I do that I don't avoid conflict. But it has got to be constructive to make any progress. Closed minds, poor listening, repeating past arguments, and standoffs don't lead to productive conflict.

Sam: Have you talked to Alan about it?

Cindy: I've tried. But he smothers me with advice and never really hears what I say. His mind is so busy with the need to control that he can't see the forest for the trees. I end up feeling guilty about my criticism. In fact, I feel guilty right now. You know I like the guys—but we're killing each other.

Sam: Well, I can't really fault anything you say. I used to have the same concerns. I tried to break it up a couple of times. Now, I guess, I'm just used to it. It's our culture and I guess we're stuck with it. We're a bunch of strong characters. Oh, the boss comes out for innovative solutions once in a while, but that lasts about one session and then we snap right back to our old ways. I used to think how great it would be if we wised up. We waste a lot of time and ideas. Most of our decisions are trade-offs. There's no commitment. And it shows! Sales are down six points. Headquarters isn't happy. The only time we seem to unite is when we have a common enemy. Maybe we should ask the human resources department for help.

Cindy: No way! The problem is ours. If we can't solve it, nobody can.

Sam: But, I can't stand here and listen to you talk about leaving.

Cindy: Well, I feel better now, but I still think I should look around. If this ship is going to sink, I don't want it on my résumé.

Sam: What do you say we both talk to Alan in the morning?

Cindy: I don't know. It needs to be brought up in front of the whole group. But I guess you're right. Alan's a good guy, but I don't think he'd be warm to a revolt.

Sam: Tell you what. You think about it overnight. I'll meet you in the coffee shop at 7:00.

Cindy: Okay, Sam, but I honestly don't see the way out of this one. Oh, look at the time! I've got to run. Thanks for listening. See you tomorrow.

This corporate environment is full of counterpunching rather than problem solving; it is in the culture as a "way of life." Constructive critique and feedback are drowned out by blaming and shouting matches. The constant fighting leads to poor decisions and compromises rather than constructive confrontation and discussion of the issues. Alan, the boss, fails to take responsibility for problem solving. Instead, he has traditionally singled out individuals, preferring to talk to them one-on-one, as a way of staying in control. The result is frustration and low morale. About the only time the group pulls together is when members face a common enemy.

It is apparent from the discussion that Cindy's team cannot agree on a common set of goals and objectives, making it virtually impossible to divide the workload in a strategically sensible way. The boss often issues job assignments by decree, without the benefit of consultation about alternative ways to handle the workload. Excellence is rarely found in such a group. More significant, however, is that this illustration is par for the course; it's standard operating procedure—their culture.

The Effect of Norms and Standards

Organization members conform to requirements placed on them, that is, the expectations of others; this is a core aspect of corporate culture. The readiness to conform is what permits regularity, order, and predictability. To adhere to group norms provides a basis for organized effort. Self-regulated conformity brings a sense of identification, belonging, and esprit de corps. On the other hand, failure to conform may stir resentment in one's colleagues and associates so that the nonconformist faces rejection and ostracism from the group. The individual may then seek to disrupt the system, preventing it from working as well as it otherwise might. Conformity itself is not good or bad. The message we are seeking to convey is that conformity may be a barrier to excellence in that it causes blindness to options. These barriers become so great that the capacity to challenge outmoded traditions, precedents, and past practices is lost. Conformity may also become an end in itself rather than a means to an end. When the dynamic of conformity is dealt with directly, the drag it produces can be reduced and creativity released for finding new and better ways of accomplishing corporate objectives.

Figure 3–1 shows how norms and standards arise under "natural" conditions. The circles at time 1 represent isolated individuals, each of whom has an opinion as to how much production is enough. The opinion is represented in numerical terms conveying the idea of "more" or "less." The numbers are diverse; at time 1, one person has an "attitude" of 15; another has an attitude of 5; in between are attitudes of 13, 10, 9, and 8.

As these people begin to interact and exchange ideas, each may feel something about his or her own attitude not in the context

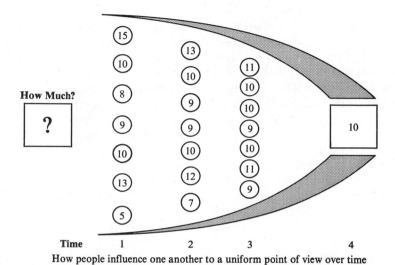

How people influence one another to a uniform point of view over time

Figure 3–1
The Dynamics of Convergence

of the issue itself but rather related to the opinions being expressed by others. The evidence can be seen more clearly at times 2 and 3. The issue itself has not changed, but people's attitudes toward it, at least in their numerical expressions, have begun to shift. The shift is anything but random. No one has gone to a more extreme position, say, 17 at the top end or 1 at the bottom. The shift is in the opposite direction; it is a tendency of people to converge around something that is intermediate. At time 4 we see the convergence process is complete. Now there is uniformity of agreement; 10 is embraced as the accepted attitude.

From a logical angle, divergence, that is, the expression of more extreme opinions, might seem to be as logical an outcome as convergence. Indeed, no shift at all might appear to be most probable. Yet this seldom happens. In a social collective, there is a strong tendency away from divergence, which is replaced instead by its opposite, that is, convergence around some end conclusion that reflects a sense of uniformity.

We can imagine what the person who is thinking 15, or 13 for that matter, is saying to him- or herself as the discussion unfolds at time 1. Such a private conversation might be, "Wow, I'm way off base on this one. I'll be seen as an eager beaver pumping for favorable attention. I'd better get in line." This kind of attitude induces pressure to conform and brings about a lowering of standards.

What about the person at 5? He or she is probably saying, at the same time, "Holy cow! I thought I was being reasonable without killing myself, but I'm way off base. I'll get the silent treatment if I don't get on board. I'd better move up."

By comparison those in the middle feel reasonably okay. They are likely to be saying to themselves, "Boy, I've really got a feel for this thing. I'll just sit tight with my reasonable point of view. I'm glad I'm not way out of line like those other guys!"

These three attitudes reveal underlying self-discussions that people might carry out in private. They are basic for any real understanding of miniature cultures of a team or macro-cultures that characterize a corporation. It is well established that such self-talk plays a large role in how people come to terms with one another.

Even more important is what happens in the aftermath of initial agreement. The agreement reached is likely to become the basis for automatic expectations. That is to say, after time 3 has been reached, it is a foregone conclusion that the ultimate basis for agreement is a 10 attitude. People are expected to go along with it—to embrace it—and to pressure each other if anyone steps out of line. If one individual fails to conform, that person becomes isolated and eventually suffers rejection as an "odd ball" or "sour puss." Such a person is seen as one who is just not with it, an individual on whom further time and effort would be wasted.

These social dynamics should not be regarded as either "good" or "bad." They are neither. It can be maintained that they are what permit people to cohere in social groups and as organizational entities. However, what can be evaluated in the perspective of "good" and "bad" is the matter of insight into the dynamics themselves and skill in managing them, *rather than be managed by them.* When taken for granted, it can be said that people are being controlled by influences outside their sphere of attention. As such, these influences are not available for examination nor subject to intelligent management. People become their victims, rather than the masters of their own fate. The result is that the company suffers needless loss of productivity.

The tendency toward convergence, described in the preceding example where members sought to group themselves around a common attitude of 10, is a major influence affecting social dynamics in corporate life today. Few social processes are more important than this tendency to conform; a uniform position becomes the "official" attitude that all members are prepared to accept and embrace, with only small variations around the theme tolerated.

A second insight can also be gained by looking back at the convergence example. In the illustration, all voices are regarded as having equal weight in determining the final position. In real life, however, some voices ultimately carry greater weight. The voice of experience is certainly listened to in a different way than is the voice of innocence. People automatically accept that experience has aided one to be more informed, and therefore an opinion offered by that individual is more worthy of attention. Likewise with the voice of authority. Other things equal, when a person in a position of authority in a group has made his or her position known, that position is accorded more significance, at least to most, even if some oppositional members feel compelled to maintain their own point of view. The general rule is that the voice of authority is acknowledged with some degree of respect, and to this degree the authority's voice carries more weight.

Another factor that exerts its influence on opinions expressed becomes particularly apparent when individuals are new to a situation. It is the voice of tradition, precedent, and past practice. The question people pose and seek to resolve is, "How did they do it, and how would they want us to do it?" Tradition, precedent, and past practice may or may not be a source of legitimate influence on how people think and shape their opinions, yet that is not the issue at hand. The issue is that tradition, precedent, and past practice do carry important weight in determining how people new to a situation are influenced in their thinking about what is right, fitting, or proper.

Social influences are all important, no less in corporate than in other aspects of social living. By and large managers have relatively little appreciation of the importance of social norms and conformity pressures. Here is an illustration of how conformity works in organization life. Take the corporate Christmas party. All the plans have been made. Conformity pressures begin to have a powerful impact on individuals who are trying to determine whether or not they should attend. Some who do not wish to partake ask themselves if they can get away with being absent. A number of questions may arise:

> "If I don't go, what will people say?"
>
> "If I go, what should I wear? How will other people be dressed?"
>
> "I don't want to miss seeing who talks with whom and if some people pair off, so I'd better go."
>
> "You can bet that Tom will find his way to Mr. Perkins and do a number on him; I don't want that to happen! In any event, I want to see for myself if Tom makes the move."

All of these can be regarded as indications of social influence related to norms and conformity pressures that dictate adherence to convention and status quo. No one wants to be out of step. Equally, no one wants a competitor to use the occasion to come up on top. Conformity behavior is powerful. People feel compelled to adhere to norms created by past social interaction. At the same time, they are determined to prevent others from taking personal or selfish advantage by opportunistically disregarding protocol.

As illustrated earlier the same phenomenon is highly evident in any production setting where norms define how much is enough. Furthermore, they underlie the fundamental issues of quality, safety, and a host of other matters. For example, zero defect in the quality area is the highest state of perfection. It is frequently pronounced as a desirable objective but rarely achieved. The actual norm or standard people come to accept is likely to be something significantly less. Other illustrations of how norms work are seen in the protocol of the executive suite, the quitting time among middle managers, or the amount of time and effort devoted to planning. The illustrations are endless.

When rigid and unbending norms of the kind being described have become widely agreed upon, the organization is caught in the grips of what we call the mechanistic era—controlled by its history and incapable of shifting to meet the requirements of the future. Just stimulating people to challenge and contest the norms and standards reflected in the status quo, however, is likely to do little more than promote controversy, increase confusion, and result in chaos. Yet the

status quo requirements must continuously be challenged in a problem-solving and creative way, not in a manner that pits person
against person to see who can win or, even worse, in a way that
results in anarchy.

In Chapter 2, we made reference to the importance of maximum commitment by all organization members to the pursuit of
corporate success through excellent performance. Additionally, we
stressed the debilitating effects on corporate vigor that result from
easy adjustments to conflict such as compromise, smoothing over,
maintaining neutrality, inducing guilt, or forcing compliance.

In the Cindy/Sam context presented earlier, counterpunching
seemed to be the norm that operated when people disagreed, with
the result that impasse and frustration came to characterize the
corporate culture. The destructive impact on teamwork was clearly
evident.

Let's return to the Cindy/Sam story for a moment, but now a
period of time has elapsed. The organization decided to undertake a
Grid OD change effort and implementation steps are well underway.
Cindy's team has learned new skills of initiative, inquiry, advocacy,
conflict solving, decision making, and critique. The quality of team
interaction is remarkably different from the illustration provided
earlier.

Sam (to Cindy): Well, let me turn back to what Cindy said for
just a minute. Cindy, are you suggesting that we continue discussion
on this topic and, as we see a problem in our interaction, that we stop
and examine it right then and there?

Cindy (to Sam): Exactly. I think it needs to be pointed out the
minute it takes place.

George (to Cindy): So we should observe each other as the
discussion goes along, looking for barriers to effective communication and problem solving. Is that right?

Cindy (to George): Yes. (*General agreement from the group.*)

Sam (to George): Let me try one on for size. George, I just
noticed that you jumped to a conclusion real fast on the Baber deal.

George (to Sam): Well, maybe I did.

Cindy (to George): Let me give you an example. As I recall, you said, "I've got the answer on this one." Then you moved the discussion right along to the next agenda item. I for one don't understand what decision was made. You go too fast for the rest of us.

George (to Cindy): I see what you mean. I've been living and sleeping with the Baber deal; I feel like I know it like the back of my hand. Let me give you some background ...

.
.
.

Sam (to George): That really clarified the situation for me. I want to corroborate what Cindy said, though. You do tend to move a little bit too fast for the rest of us when we start off on a new topic.

George (to group): I appreciate the feedback and, seriously, I understand what you're saying. I'll try to be aware of that but if and when you see me doing it again, just point it out, right when it happens, like Cindy said.

The discussion recounted above could not have taken place in the team that existed prior to engaging in a major effort to shift the organization's culture to one that increased the potential for productive and effective interaction.

Corporate Commitment

Strong leaders are often identified with greatness, accomplishment, and causes that are morally and intellectually sound. Patriotism is identification with a nation and its actions. Loyalty is identification with a cause or a person. A dedicated individual tends to be mature and healthy. It seems logical that a corporation would seek to earn the dedicated commitment of its members. What are the conditions for doing so? Corporate commitment and dedication come when people feel a stake in the outcome of their endeavors. They feel committed to objectives and responsible for results, realizing that their efforts have an impact and make a difference. To manage the culture of a business, people must comprehend and effectively manage the conditions that promote involvement, commitment, and dedication.

Some corporations achieve a high degree of identification with organization performance goals throughout their membership. This identification is evident among members in their positive morale and personal commitment of efforts toward corporate excellence. It is a sound foundation of corporate health. It is present when effort is widespread and concentrated on corporate achievement. In other corporations, morale and commitment at a high level is less evident. People "feel good about the company," but this is because they feel secure rather than because they have personally contributed to its success. In still others, apathy and indifference replace morale, commitment, and dedication as descriptions of the existing corporate climate. In still another group of companies, great commitment to achievement by some, with equally great hidden resentments among others, provides evidence of behavioral dynamics associated with authority/obedience ways of managing. In some companies morale is high because the people are treated well. Good relations are maintained at the expense of corporate effectiveness. This kind of identification with a nurturing organization that gives much and asks for little in return is bound to produce a loss of vigor and a complacency that is the antithesis of excellence. Corporate welfarism is no less debilitating than is custodial treatment of healthy people in other walks of life. Finally, some organizations are characterized by a culture that rewards people when they behave and do as they are told, staying in their places like obedient children. On the other hand, when these "youngsters" fall out of line, punishment ensues. Such management practices often foster great loyalty from their membership, but the adverse side of this is inordinate dependency and an inability to exercise self-responsibility and initiative.

People—The Wellsprings of Corporate Energy

It is one thing to recognize that change may be essential to the achievement of corporate excellence. It is quite a different matter to do something about it. The bridge that can carry an organization from recognition to action is in *people* whose interactions at any point in time are culture-bound. For the culture to change, people must change.

Human energy is what powers every corporate achievement. Corporate excellence on paper is nothing more than a statement of good intentions until human energy is applied through the exercise of business skills and judgment. For one individual to deal with another effectively, he or she must comprehend and act on at least three issues: human motivation, uses and abuses of power and authority, and the manner in which conformity dynamics influence the way people think and feel. Without a basic understanding of these issues and skill in using them, boundless energies otherwise available remain locked up or are at best only partially released. The full potential is left unrealized. "Striving" for corporate soundness becomes "driving" for corporate soundness, and, no matter how well intended, "driving" produces resistance to change in the form of antagonisms—feelings of being taken advantage of, being walked on, exploited, or left out. Pressuring for change by asking people to reject current norms only ensures that this major barrier to corporate excellence, resistance to change, which seems always present to some degree, is not eliminated or overcome. Indeed, the barrier of resentment may loom ever greater.

Many companies have endeavored to improve themselves without taking advantage of these insights into the dynamics of behavior. Some chief executives and many managers as well assume that barriers to excellence are found on the business side of the business only. Usually, problems *are* on the business side of the business in that problems of the corporation undoubtedly show up in operational difficulties. However, the reasons for the operational difficulties are most likely to be human in character and origin and to be centered in involvement, commitment, and dedication to solving problems. Culture can support or work against these evolutions that lie behind the effort. Exerting pressure to improve operational results without resolving the human impediments that cause operational limitations is but a treatment of the symptoms. The real malady persists.

A foundation to operational excellence lies in the comprehension and use of a model for what constitutes excellence in problem-solving behavior. When people have acquired problem-solving skills in their human interactions, these skills can be used to eliminate and confront operational barriers to excellence.

Summary

When a company enables its members to manage themselves and one another in 9,9 ways, it is using and practicing sound principles of human behavior. It is creating a culture that promotes relationships among people leading to two fundamental consequences. One is that individuals can be mature, adult, and ready to accept the challenge to achieve objectives to which they can openly commit themselves. The other is that since these objectives to which they have committed themselves are aligned with the profitability purposes of the firm, the company is mobilizing human resources in such a way as to realize its aims as well. Self-interests and corporate interests are meshed.

Achieving sound behavior dynamics as a first step in organization development is key for mobilizing the wellsprings of human energy potentially available. Excellence predicated on sound corporate logic and the implementation of valid business skills and techniques is not likely to be achieved in situations where conflict is not faced, where creativity is stifled by blind conformity, and where people lack a sound approach to critique and learning. The critical ingredient—motivated people who are knowledgeable about managing such social dynamics—is missing. Creating a corporate culture that pursues excellence through mobilizing the energies of people and bringing the behavioral dynamics of the firm under insightful management significantly increases the likelihood of its accomplishment.

4

Organization Diagnosis

The previous chapters have provided some illustrations of what is currently known as to the character of behavior typical in organizations today. The range and depth of abuses of human resources in organization interactions are apparent in a number of the examples and case studies presented. Only the 9,9 approach provides a description of ideal modeling as it relates to the human side of organization. The other Grid theories represent distortions of sound behavior in varying degrees in the sense that they prevent full human resource effectiveness from emerging. This is because styles other than 9,9 create contradictions between fulfilling the needs of the organization and satisfying the needs of people; therefore, they sacrifice one to the other (this is true of 9,1 and 1,9) or they seek to balance the two concerns in some fashion (5,5 and paternalism) or they give up altogether (1,1). Only the 9,9 style treats the potential for integration of the two concerns in a way that fully focuses and concentrates human resources on accomplishing organization purpose.

The goal of organization development is to aid organization members to gain a model of sound behavior and to compare it with what actually transpires among people who work together. This is the ideal/actual model approach. It offers any manager a comparison between what is possible and what is actual. It opens up a gap between the two. Intellectual gaps such as the one being described can become strong motivators of change. They demonstrate the existence of a discrepancy in human performance that is adverse to productivity, creativity, innovation, profitability, and long-term continuity.

Being able to see and experience gaps then is a first operational step toward the introduction of change. However, we all live so closely tied to the actual world that we find it hard to break away in order to see what is possible. Organization diagnosis provides alternative methods of data gathering that can help people recognize and "measure" the seriousness of these discrepancies as a first step in planned change. These four methods of organization diagnosis are described in the following sections.

Key Approaches to Organization Diagnosis

Diagnosis of business practices may lead to the identification of needed improvements that can be implemented in a routine way. Quite often, they are within the grasp of competent managers who are currently part of the corporation's staff. Sometimes, however, the problems of the corporation that show up in operational difficulties are human in character and origin. Measures taken to improve results without resolving the human resource impediments that are causing the operational limitations merely treat the symptoms. When people have acquired problem-solving skills in their human interactions, these same skills can then be used to confront and eliminate barriers to operational excellence. The point is that the business logic itself may be sound, but the corporation may need to view its difficulties in this area as symptoms of a deeper, underlying problem that resides in the realm of human resources.

Accurate diagnosis is as critical in organization development as it is in medicine. The greater the insight into the core human problems of the organization, the greater the likelihood of being able to design and implement strategies for solving them so as to strengthen business practices.

Generally speaking, there are six behavioral areas within which organization difficulties may be indicated. They are

1. Power/Authority,
2. Norms/Standards,
3. Cohesion/Morale,
4. Differentiation/Structure,
5. Goals/Objectives, and
6. Feedback/Critique.

Digging out areas of difficulty in each of these six dimensions provides a basis for taking the next steps. The first word in each pair is looking at the area from a psychological point of view, whereas the second term is used when that area is viewed from a sociological perspective. Both are needed to convey these two closely allied thoughts. Together they serve to buttress the depth and comprehensiveness of whatever observations are made.

The goal of behavioral diagnosis is clear, but how do we go about it? There are four major ways and a variety of minor approaches. None of them is mutually exclusive, and no one approach is better than the others. A combination of all may represent the soundest approach because the findings from one diagnostic procedure can be cross-validated against the findings from others. The four diagnostic methodologies include

1. Interviewing,

2. In situ diagnosis,

3. Simulation, and

4. Participant observation.

In *interviewing,* a representative sample of the corporation's membership is engaged in discussion, usually by consultants seeking a perspective on how the company appears to be operating. This method can be regarded as objective in the sense that the consultants have no particular vested interest in a specific outcome. Interviewing can also be undertaken by an inside/outside combination of consultants, with one acting as a guide to the other. In this case the insider provides steering and background information and acts as a sounding board for interpreting findings. The outsider contributes his or her unique strategies of inquiry. The fact that many companies are now employing professionally trained and academically qualified OD experts is increasingly blurring the distinction between outsider and insider status.

In *in situ diagnosis,* experts who are on the scene often have the opportunity to observe unusual and critical events and to gain deep insight on how they are dealt with as the problems unfold. This observational diagnosis allows the experts to go beyond what people report they do and to observe how they actually interact in dealing with the problem at hand. In *simulation,* organization members reenact their typical ways of performing some planning or problem-solving activity, making it possible for the experts to "read between the lines" as the activity is being enacted. In *participant observation* an outsider(s) joins a corporation or one of its components for an extended period of time, say, one or two months or even longer. During this period the expert is provided free and full access to whatever activities he or she may wish to study and without any responsibilities for influencing the observed events. At the end of the assignment, the consultant(s) is in an informed position to provide a diagnostic review of the underlying dynamics observed to be characteristic of the corporation and to suggest developmental approaches by which they might be strengthened or changed.

Of the four methodologies, interviewing and in situ diagnosis can have an immediate impact on the organization. In the first, as the interviews are conducted, those being interviewed quickly gain understanding, either by reviewing what they have been asked or by reviewing their interview experience with others who are being similarly interviewed. The mere fact of what the interviewer(s) attends to and what he or she seems to discount or to place less importance upon can have an impact on the members. They may immediately emphasize activities they perceive to be important to the interviewer(s) and may treat nominally those activities interpreted as insignificant. The distortions, however, are not great because the character of the required changes is usually of larger magnitude than the internal members could readily introduce by themselves.

In situ diagnosis is different, however, and in a certain sense constitutes a more penetrating intervention. This is because the observer(s) relies on his or her observations as the basis for challenging and confronting participants as they experience the event, though it may also be introduced after they have engaged in resolving the episode. Thus, from the critique, participants can immediately examine any discrepancies between how they experienced and interpreted the event and how the consultant(s) perceived it. This can significantly affect their interpretation of that episode and how they might expect to handle similar ones.

Simulations seem to have a lesser degree of impact at least in the eyes of those who participate in the ongoing situation. This is because they are serving as guinea pigs without necessarily having concern for the conclusions reached. However, the findings may have a powerful impact when reported to those responsible for decision making. This is partly because a simulation tends to accentuate certain qualities, becoming somewhat like a caricature of the real event, and this permits the identification of underlying pulls and tugs that otherwise remain obscure.

In participant observation, any conclusions the outside consultant draws are automatically withheld until some future time. But, when reported, they can be very impactful because of the sheer weight of evidence that can be drawn upon to deepen awareness. The generalization remains true, however, that any consultant(s) investigating internal organization affairs can influence the very events that have been topics of observation and review.

Historically, participant observation had its roots in field work conducted by comparative anthropologists. Their goal was to understand how the culture they were observing operated without contaminating or influencing it in either an adverse or positive way. This, of course, is not entirely possible as their sheer presence immediately introduces an extraneous variable into the situation. However, the point is that while participant observation is underway, the consultant(s) seeks to exercise minimal influence, focusing attention on gathering data to gain an accurate reading of the event and in this way providing meaningful conclusions in the aftermath.

Each of these four diagnostic methodologies is illustrated in an abbreviated case study with specific comments. A number of useful tactics for making them as successful as possible also are provided.

Interviewing

Interviewing is an obvious methodology and undoubtedly the one we rely on most often. One of its advantages is that we can evaluate conclusions from one interview in the light of findings from others. Without detailing the skills involved in the interviewing process, it may be useful to indicate some of the ground rules we seek to implement when undertaking a diagnostic interview strategy.

1. We start at the top of the organization diagnosis unit, sampling all other levels, functions, and so on, including wage and hourly personnel.

2. The number of people interviewed depends, of course, on the size of the organization. The idea is to interview as many people as necessary to obtain a sound representative sample. In most companies we work with at least 25 or 30 people on a one-to-one basis. The number

rises accordingly with the time available and the number of group interviews done in conjunction with solo interviews.

3. The general timeframe within which we operate is one to two weeks.

4. Optimally, interviews are conducted at the interviewee's place of work rather than asking the interviewee to come to some temporary office or to meet the consultant off site.

5. The interviews are scheduled for no less than 45 minutes to one hour. In the case of higher level people or key organization members and in group interviews, more time may be desirable.

6. Notes are taken for later reference regarding specific agenda items, potential points of interpersonal or intergroup conflict, and so on. A one-line physical description of the interviewee (estimated age, hair color, weight, features such as glasses, beard, and so on) may help you recapture the image of the person when you review the specific content of what was said.

7. A period of free time is scheduled between interviews to record as much detail as possible and to process what has been heard. This focuses attention on key issues and highlights new points of inquiry for the next interview.

8. The interviews are conducted by pairs or trios of interviewers whenever possible. This allows for the diagnostic team to discuss and interpret findings from each interview, to locate one another's blind spots, and to identify what remains to be learned.

9. A number of group interviews may be conducted with membership drawn from one level in order to study candor, spontaneity, breadth and quality of participation. Interviews composed of peer groups often prove a very rich source of information because members stimulate one another and new issues and opinions can surface.

10. We rely on leads from the interviewee rather than using an arbitrary sequence of questions, but we do have a structured format in mind to ensure that all key areas are covered.

11. We avoid offering helpful suggestions or leading the interview based on an assumption about where it might go. Suggestions may be appropriate later, but the goal of diagnostic interviewing is to learn without biasing the audience.

12. We keep the interview centered on process (behavioral) issues rather than on content (business practices) concerns as much as possible, but seek out the connections between the two.

13. We make it a rule not to quote to any interviewee what some other interviewee has said. On the other hand, we also do not offer anonymity. If confidentiality is requested, we explore the individual's reasons for wanting it. Rarely does this come up and when it does, the requests are usually withdrawn after discussion. The underlying premise is to promote openness and candor in the organization rather than to stifle it.

14. We test the limits of the interviewee before concluding an interview. This means asking about issues thought to be relevant that may not yet have been touched upon.

15. A final review takes place at the top to summarize learnings and offer guidance and direction in areas of needed or potential improvement.

16. We write a detailed summary for our own back-home files. This helps to promote learning and also provides rich clinical material for later study. The summary should identify common themes, weight problem areas as to importance, and suggest how to feed the findings back to the organization.

Systematic Critique

Once the interviews are completed and findings summarized, the pertinent issue is always, "How can these data now be made available to the organization in such a way as to ensure understanding, insight, and readiness to take the next steps toward solving outstanding problems?" This was raised in interviewing rule 15 in the preceding section. A summary of guidelines we seek to implement during this feedback session is as follows:

1. We present the feedback to the entire top team, not to the CEO alone and not to each member on a one-to-one basis.

2. We present the data in a discussion format as opposed to a formal or written report. The presentation brings forth discussion that may reveal new reactions, interpretations, rationalizations, and defensive thinking. These can then be met head on rather than allowing such negative attitudes to become sources of rejection and discontent. If requested, a written summary statement may be provided later.

3. We schedule the final critique session to extend over a continuous four-hour period. If possible, we schedule the critique session on the final day of the interviewing process with another session to be held two or three days later to answer any new questions and to introduce and discuss the next steps.

4. In this final session, we respect the anonymity of sources. We tell what has been learned but not from whom. This question rarely arises, but if it does, we answer it with the following rationale: "What we have learned may be important but from whom we have learned it is not particularly pertinent." This protects the anonymity of sources, even though it has not been promised. Maintaining anonymity in this case is important because someone in the top team may use what is said about lower organization members against them.

5. If required, we arrange an additional personal discussion with the CEO. This makes it possible for the top person to review his or her situation without the open involvement of the entire team.

6. We avoid promising a successful outcome, but rather we seek informed consent by pointing out alternative actions that can be evaluated with respect to the next steps being recommended.

7. We introduce possible side effects, if any, and suggest ways in which they can be avoided through the design of an overall strategy.

8. We have one member of the diagnostic team lead the feedback discussion, but all members are to be present and to participate by supplementing what is being said and offering additional examples as appropriate.

The following are excerpts from real-life interviews undertaken within a client company during a three-day organization diagnosis project. These interviews were completed as the initial step in a full-fledged Grid Organization Development project with the next steps already in place, that is, an Executive Grid Seminar and a Team Building project to be undertaken by the top team. The parts we have extracted for purposes of illustration primarily concern the dynamics of leadership within this particular organization.

Interview 1

Robert Smith, Manager, Management & Organization Development

Smith reports to the Director of Human Resources. Smith was commissioned to be our guide and to set up the interview schedule for us. One of our consultants chatted with him previously about expectations for the interview sessions. Apparently Smith mentioned to interviewees that our primary focus was to orient them to the upcoming seminar. This was not our original intent, but the expectation had nevertheless been created, so we worked with this in mind.

State of the Business

When we asked about last year's results, Smith reported a dramatic financial gain for the operation, so much so that domestic results exceeded all other international operations. Domestic had moved from eighth position to first position during this period. The first two quarters' targets were met, and during the second two quarters, operational results surpassed projected targets with a 57 percent productivity gain over the preceding year. These results are perceived by the organization as being led and directed by the CEO, John Carter. Carter's new objective, now that last year's results are in, is to maintain this number one position.

The three-year plan represents a growth orientation in terms of productivity, sales, and investment strategy. Another key issue is to establish an "extrovert" image for the company as it positions itself against external competition, the largest, of course, being XYZ Corporation. When we described XYZ's new plans to flatten the hierarchy and rid itself of bureaucratic decision making, Smith said, "Oh, it sounds like they're trying to do what we're trying to do in terms of getting more creative decision making lower down in the organization." When we discussed another competitor, Smith recognized them as outstanding, particularly in the area of managing human resources. He commented that his own human resources department and that of all the company had a long way to go to become as creative in its approach to deploying people.

View of the Top Man

Smith said that if you were to sit down and have a drink with Carter, the story would go something like this. "Yeah, I've heard it all before and it looks real nice on paper. But the fact of the matter is that this teamwork business is soft stuff." According to Smith, Carter likes to get into the nitty-gritty details of things himself, and this sometimes stands in the way of lower level decision making. A significant illustration of this is that Carter has no reservations in swooping down into lower levels of the organization to procure the data or to enlist a subordinate to propagandize key pieces of data in his behalf. This is often threatening to some of Carter's direct reports as they never know when Carter will "swoop" and, in so doing, undermine their authority. Carter has a good understanding of all the working pieces of the organization. He possesses an ability to look at detailed financial reports of one little minuscule division and to comprehend the big picture dynamics contained therein. In a sense this reinforces his command over the company as a whole.

Smith communicated the feeling that Carter is starting to build some degree of trust and respect with his own direct reports and is seen less as a dictator than in the past. For instance, he has accorded a greater degree of respect to his financial director who was among those responsible for the past year's success, having contributed over 50 percent of the operating revenues for the company. This, of course, was key to Carter's success as well.

John Carter, according to Smith, manages on a one-to-one basis—the old divide-and-conquer routine, in the sense that there is no open debate or critique among the other top team reports. Carter deals with each one individually. Smith told us that the top reports do not feel they are a team; rather, when they have a meeting, they are competitive with one another in a negative or put-down way, all vying for "Dad's" attention. They meet weekly and if one person makes a statement that contains an error or, say, misspells a word on a flipchart, the others laugh and chide him so that he is seen as less than fully competent.

As a result of the previous interview with Smith, we formulated a preamble for use in subsequent interviews. This included a statement of our objectives organized into three categories:

1. To provide some background rationale for doing prestudy material for the upcoming seminar.
2. To chat with those people scheduled to attend the seminar to better understand the current dynamics of the company.
3. To review expectations for what the seminar and subsequent follow-up might achieve for the organization as a whole. This was in line with expectations already held by interviewees; however, our intent was to delve much deeper into the leadership dynamics impacting organization culture.

Interview 2

Jack Williams, Executive Assistant to the President

Jack sits in an important position as executive assistant to the top man. Although he was not scheduled as a probable participant in the upcoming executive program, we thought it useful to hear his perspective. He was a personable fellow, perhaps in his mid-thirties. He came on board with the company as a branch manager and had accepted his current position as a way of broadening his experience within the organization. He feels the decision was mutual. That is, he wanted to get into something new and move up the ladder, but John Carter wanted to check him out, so to speak, and challenged him to sit in the office next door so as to prove himself.

Perspective on the Top Team

Williams participates in executive committee meetings. Prior to taking his current position, he updated himself on current issues through the careful and deliberate study of minutes from past meetings. He feels there is no communication at the top. The report he gave us was similar to what we had heard from many others in that each person reports from his own area, and John Carter rules on what is happening. Other team members do not comment on what is said by their colleagues. Carter's direct reports often fail to report issues at the executive committee meetings in order to avoid a public cross-examination, preferring instead to bring the issues to Carter for discussion on a one-to-one basis.

According to Williams, Carter speaks with conviction about the need for teamwork but his egotistical nature is a great barrier to achieving it. He provided us with an example of a presentation to be made in the next few days by the liaison person regarding a particular project. This project is to be reviewed and adjusted by Carter prior to presentation but is not to be distributed among others, i.e., salespeople, for their review and critique. We tested whether it would be of any value to have people from other divisions test it, and Williams responded positively. He said that from a technical point of view there could be some improvement, but the bigger issue was that by shutting out input from these significant others, no shared objectives were formed and motivation to implement the project was low. Interestingly enough, at lunch we discussed this matter with another interviewee and discovered that there are some portions of the bonus system funded by overall company performance, so there does indeed exist a common objective for those who carry out such projects as the one described above. Despite this, however, the feeling that runs rampant through the organization is much as Williams described it, and the result tends to be low morale and stifled initiative.

In this particular interview-based organization diagnosis effort, we concluded our work with a feedback and critique session with the entire top team. Carter indicated reluctance to be involved, preferring instead to receive a written report for his perusal. He was inclined to believe that there were no teamwork problems; rather, he looked for a solution within the realm of business logic. Upon reflection, however, he did see the value in hearing us out on what we had learned about the organization in order to gain deeper insight on how others in his top team perceived him as a leader.

Following the critique and feedback session with the top team, Carter expressed an interest in a final one-to-one session with us. This wrap-up session took place as the very final diagnostic activity, after all other group sessions had been concluded. Carter insisted on such a meeting. We felt his underlying rationale was that he felt dissatisfied with our conclusions in contrast to his own interpretations. In other words, having been confronted by the data we presented, he felt it important to present to us his own version of one critical event in particular. The unique advantage is that this offered us the opportunity to provide him with a picture of this event as it had been seen by others and reported to us. This permitted him to test his own interpretation of the event in comparison with our rendition of what had transpired.

Wrap-up Session with Carter

Feedback and Critique to the CEO

As is true of so many chief executives, the "classical" problem of getting into organization development first had to be overcome in these discussions with John Carter.

As our conversations got underway, Carter had no reluctance to accept the premise that his leadership had been that of running a one-man show. He then went on to explain why: "The level of business skills among the members of this company is so low that I find myself more and more the mastermind, thinking out the business strategy issues that others should be fully capable of providing for themselves but are not. This leads me to challenge the conclusions reached by you and your colleagues. You seem to feel I am adverse to teamwork, participation, collaboration, and mutuality. However, that's not true, though I can see how others might have perceived it this way.

"Let me give you an example of how I operate and why.

"Recently, I asked my key people to develop alternative propositions for a new headquarters in the downtown area. Upon completion, I received a proposal and organized five visits with them to the recommended sites. At the top of their list was a site in the highest priced real estate center in the city, while the one they had deemed least acceptable lay on the periphery of town. This latter possibility, however, was highly desirable from the standpoint of providing adequate space for facilities, reasonable access, and so forth. Additionally, the price tag on this option had not gone sky high.

"After seeing the sites, and still keeping my conclusions to myself, I asked them to review with me once again their underlying rationale for the priority of their recommendations. This they did. At that point, I told them I disagreed with the manner in which they had ranked the options. I made it quite clear that the quality of economic analysis on their part left much to be desired, indicating that they had failed to have a long-term perspective in completing their analysis, overlooking the risks and benefits of site selection ten and fifteen and twenty years down the road, a period of time when I expect we will still be housed in the quarters that we select today. At that point I told them that the site they had given the lowest priority to seemed optimal to me, based on the initial criteria we had discussed."

After he completed this story, Carter turned to me and said, "So now you can plainly see why they think I run a one-man show. What I have described is only an example of a single case, but the same thing seems to be true of every situation, regardless of the stakes. This is why I am convinced that any training effort we undertake needs to focus on business practices rather than on executive teamwork. I see no reason to automatically assume this is a teamwork problem when there exist such vivid illustrations of how faulty business practices are leading us astray."

As a group, we responded to him as follows. We told him that we had heard the other side of the same story. That version said that the selection committee had in fact reached the same decision as Carter regarding optimal site selection but had then concluded among themselves that Carter would never settle for less than the most prestigious, high-priced, central city location. Therefore they disregarded the economics of the situation and painted in the picture they thought Carter would want to see.

We told him, "It is for this reason that the problem lies more in the area of teamwork than sound business practices. They knew and reached an objective conclusion that concurs with your own regarding the best site from an economics and business perspective. It was only in trying to double-think you that they discounted their own economic analysis and inserted a new political priority. As long as the politics of acceptance and rejection, approval and disapproval, and avoiding the adverse consequences of rejection have a significant impact on the recommendations people make, then a severe and enduring difficulty of teamwork is present and, moreover, affects bottom-line performance. The needed openness and candor, confrontation, and facing up to conflict simply isn't there, and no amount of training in business analysis and business practices will suffice to solve the problem."

This caught his attention. We went on to outline numerous other key points from the interviews. Finally, he asked for time to reflect. Three days later, he gave his endorsement for the upcoming seminar, adding that he wanted an extended activity at a later time to deal with the teamwork issue in his executive group. He expressed his conviction to start at the top, with his involvement, in the hope of having this new development effort cascade down through all levels of the organization. This is an approach to which we heartily subscribe.

The example clearly draws a distinction introduced earlier in this chapter. The competence to make decisions based on sound business practices was indeed present in this company. However, the failure to use it existed in faulty human resource practices. The latter had to be resolved before the former could be implemented. In significant ways, this parallels the problem represented in Chapter 1 with regard to human effectiveness in the cockpit.

General Findings

On the basis of conducting many diagnostic sessions according to the guidelines cited earlier, it can be said that:

1. Power/Authority issues usually stand at the forefront of barriers to corporate effectiveness. Until these barriers have been confronted and dealt with, it is unlikely that change efforts aimed at Norms/Standards, Cohesion/Morale, Differentiation/Structure, Goals/Objectives, or Feedback/Critique will have meaningful impact or be of enduring quality.

2. Organization members experience the interviews and systematic critique session as interesting, provocative, and rewarding. This is so even when the conclusions are troublesome and difficult to accept.

3. Interviewers who focus on real issues that are of importance to the effectiveness of the organization earn respect and establish credibility for really digging into the heart of problems. Key executives look forward to having us lead an open discussion of findings. It is rare for anyone not to participate, and it is common for the systematic critique session to be active with much give and take. If necessary to overcome initial hesitation, we focus attention away from our findings and concentrate on impediments in the group's own "here-and-now" behavior before returning to the "big picture."

4. This kind of diagnostic interviewing provides the organization with a baseline from which future progress can be assessed.

5. We conclude with a face-to-face discussion with the top team It is important to ensure understanding and to "be there" to work through reservations and doubts rather than letting them fester to produce resentment and resis-

tance to change. Fully informed understanding is essential to moving forward with the next steps. A written report may be supplied to the CEO after this final consultation has taken place.

With regard to the final point, our conclusions might have been reported to all those interviewed, but more often than not it is the top team alone to whom our findings are given. The rationale is as follows.

The sample of those interviewed often represents several levels, usually a diagonal slice of the corporation. When such a group is assembled, particularly when there has been no prior training and development, such a gathering calls for lower status persons to speak up in the presence of higher status individuals. Ideally there should be free and open exchange among several levels and across different functions, but frequently there is not. Indeed, that may be a significant portion of the difficulties the organization is encountering. It has seemed unfair to put people on the spot in this way, and particularly so when top leaders all too often hear what they are told but interpret it in a paternalistic framework, feeling compelled to tell lower levels why they are "wrong." The lower levels may not be in error in any objective sense, but being told that they are only serves to perpetuate and strengthen the attitude that it is unwise to speak up in the presence of one's superiors.

In contrast, we have reported back to the whole group from time to time. On such occasions, it has often met with success, especially when we have had the opportunity to meet in advance with the top team to clarify that their role is not to explain or to correct comments made by lower levels. Rather, the objective is to listen, understand, and feel free to pose further inquiries in order to gain improved understanding for what lower levels are really trying to communicate.

Offering Recommendations

Since Power/Authority seems almost universally to be the central problem, we usually try to pose this issue in Grid terms. The rationale is that the Grid characterizes all major Power/Authority issues and shows comparatively the options that can contribute to conflict resolution.

In the sense it is being employed here, the Managerial Grid, in other words, is a "Power Grid." It identifies different ways by which power is likely to be exercised in any organization and aids organization members to appreciate the consequences of executives, managers, or supervisors from using their power and authority in optional ways. Some of these options are capable of turning people on and inducing involvement and commitment; others may generate antagonism and hostility; and still others produce indifference and apathetic withdrawal. Engaging in such analysis as a hands-on, direct learning experience sets the stage for what follows.

The remaining phases of Grid Development are based on empirical findings as to the most common sequence for solving problems present in organization after organization. These are reviewed with the top team, and interview findings are correlated to them for illustration and for strengthening the motivation to grapple with them.

Contrary to common belief, the stages of organization-wide Grid Development, that is, Grid Seminar learning (Phase 1), Team Building (Phase 2), Interface Conflict Solving (Phase 3), Ideal Strategic Corporate Modeling (Phase 4), Tactical Implementation of the Model (Phase 5), and Stabilization (Phase 6), are not a fixed and inviolate sequence. However, they are a natural sequence. Systematic Power/Authority insights from the Grid Seminar strengthen the Team Building effort. Team Building in turn paves the way for Interface Conflict Solving. With these three problem areas under control, that is, individual, team, and intergroup relationships, it then becomes possible for the top team to work together toward redesigning the corporation as a Phase 4 activity. It is not unusual, however, for the entire sequence to be shifted and reordered. The most common shift is to start with Interface Conflict Solving, followed by Grid Seminar learning, and so on. The reason for this shift is that in many organizations, the intergroup conflicts are so intense that other problems are dwarfed by comparison.

Interviewing can be a key way of measuring what is actually going on in a corporation, but there are numerous other methods as well.

In Situ Diagnosis

This approach to diagnosis is one that takes advantage of the consultant being present during a fast-moving crisis situation (in situ) which, upon closer examination, reveals barriers to corporate effectiveness. Again, the most common conclusion is that Power/Authority is the root source of corporate malaise.

In situ diagnosis is less disruptive than interviewing during the period in which the episode is in progress. The consultant, who usually is not actively participating, is likely to be disregarded or ignored. In the aftermath, however, the consultant uses what has been observed as the basis for helping the organization diagnose how it is in fact conducting itself, particularly when the chips are down.

The following was written immediately upon completion of an in situ diagnostic opportunity. We had been invited into the organization to conduct an interview-based diagnosis. The situation is that the company headquarters and two of its major plants (WFE and YXO) are located in the same place. The plants are in different lines of business and were seen as having little in common, save for sharing some staff services between them.

The Picket Line Crisis

Robertson, a corporate VP who had been asked to take charge of the WFE plant on a temporary basis, was to pick me up at 7:40 A.M. for my appointment with Joe Perkins, but he was late. When I got in the car, he apologized and said, "We have a real emergency. We're being picketed. I don't know the entire story, but it looks like we're in for some real trouble."

He went on to say, "The picket line is not our union, but rather is one that represents several other plants in the area. We don't know why we are being picketed or what the complaint is. We do know that our union is ignorant of what is going on. Furthermore, we don't know what kind of picket it is, but this could be very bad because we have five hundred delivery trucks coming in per 24-hour day, and if they don't show up and can't bring in raw materials, we can't get on with the conversion process—and that's crucial."

We had two options for getting into the plant—the 42nd Street gate used by the YXO plant or the 45th Street entrance used by WFE. We entered via the 45th Street gate. Ten or twelve pickets were marching in close formation. Each had a printed sign. The weather was cold and everyone had on coats and hats. It was a moment of drama to see Robertson nudge his car through the line, almost scraping people on either side but with no contact made. I was so busy watching the event that I didn't pay much attention to what was displayed on the signs. I don't think Robertson did either.

When we got to his office, I anchored myself to a chair by his desk and remained there for the next three hours, not budging one way or the other, with the result that I had a window to every moment of the drama. During this period, the telephone rang and people appeared, disappeared, and reappeared. Robertson was totally at the center of decision making, with others primarily supplying information, venturing very few opinions or options, and contributing little or nothing by way of judgment or interpretation.

There were a number of key players in the act. They showed up more or less spontaneously and then later made their exit. Ben Taylor, the manager of the YXO plant, and John Walker, Taylor's director of human resources, are the important names to recall. A participant on the telephone was Peter Todd, someone located downstate but apparently not a member of the company.

They still didn't know what kind of a picket line this was, what the protest was about, how long it might last, its impact on operations, and so on. I will try to recount something of each of these.

Gathering Factual Data

The greatest problem, which lasted about an hour, was that no one could clearly establish what kind of picket it was. In many conversations on the phone, Robertson characterized it as illegal, whether or not it was informational, because the line was interrupting trucks from entering the plant. He kept announcing to people that a principle was involved and that there should be no negotiation or contact with the union whatsoever because it would indicate collusion, regardless of whether it was a strike against the plant or whether it constituted some other complaint. Robertson referred to it as a strike situation in a number of his telephone conversations. Use of the word "strike" added fuel to the fire, although he routinely tended to correct it at a later time. This seemed to harden attitudes, making it more difficult for people to interact with Robertson in an open, problem-probing sense. It was evident that inquiry was low since no one had read the signs coming through and no one was willing to go out to take a picture although Robertson had a camera in his drawer. The system did little insofar as utilizing the resources available to it. Advocacy was virtually nonexistent, and conflicts and tensions beneath the surface had no opportunity to express themselves. Furthermore, there was no effort at critique of what was going on and little focus on reconstructing the events as they finally came to be known at the end.

The Issue

It turned out to be an informational picket, as contrasted with a union picket. A union picket is one in which the picket line is something that other union members are expected to respect and therefore not to cross. An informational picket only announces in a public way that the location is engaged in a practice that has been judged inappropriate or unsafe. There is no intent to shut down operations by isolating the location and making it inoperable. It took an exceedingly long time to establish this fact, however.

As far as I can construct it, the issue was that both YXO and WFE contracted with a housekeeping organization for cleaning services. These services are being performed by nonunion personnel for a much lower rate than could be done by outside union people and certainly by company employees. The employees net approximately $10/hour plus 42 percent in extra benefits, so they are paid around $15/hour. The cleaning people are paid about $6/hour with no additional benefits. Therefore the services can be provided at roughly one-third the expense of utilizing union personnel. Furthermore, the nonunion people are described as "really on the hustle, working an extremely hard day"—in other words, they are hungry for a dollar rather than complacent in the sense of moving at the snail's pace that seems to typify company employees. All in all, I think that the picket offensive was not so much aimed at the company as at the independent contractor for his failure to respect the union and employ union personnel to do the work.

The Key

If there is a key element to the entire situation, it is Peter Todd, the independent contractor.

Another organization represented by a man named Pearson has been competing with the first housekeeping company for these contracts. The contender has consistently been on the short end of the bidding. Pearson, who apparently represents yet another union, is thought to have inspired the picket. My understanding was that this was done to gain company attention in a pressure sense for future use. This became apparent when YXO legal personnel and the official union legal representatives finally got together mid-morning and let it be known that Pearson would be willing to meet with Robertson during the afternoon if a meeting could take place entirely off the record. Such a meeting was convened.

The Other Plant Manager

During the morning there were several conversations between Taylor, the other plant manager, and Robertson. The primary issue was to avoid clustering the pickets at one gate or the other. However, a support contingent arrived before Robertson could prevent this, and they clustered at the WFE entrance. The other issue was to ensure that police protection was provided at any picketed gate. This is where the depth of the interface between the two plants became apparent.

Taylor and his people had arranged for the pickets to be concentrated at the WFE gate. This was based on the automatic premise that whatever the union was protesting had to do with WFE and not YXO. The labor lawyer had been in favor of concentrating the pickets at the WFE gate as he, too, had automatically assumed that the problem was located there. This became a win/lose battle in numerous ways. It could not have been more gorgeously programmed for insight into how interfaces emerge.

At this point, Robertson had a call from someone in the public relations area at the YXO plant. He was preparing a news release "just in case." The news release emphasized the spontaneous rather than deliberate way that WFE was the target of the picket effort. All of these groups, i.e., the YXO plant manager, the human resources and labor people, indicated the depth of interface tensions between YXO and WFE. They were immeasurably deep, widespread, and spontaneously felt. The question was, "Why?" The answer that repeatedly came back was, "Robertson."

Robertson is a very tough-minded, hard-boiled, dollar-conscious, bottom-line executive who has made every effort to stiffen the backs of the YXO plant as well as to stiffen the backs of people in his own outfit in terms of bargaining. He has communicated his tough stance not only through wage negotiations but in many other ways such as taking work away from the unions through independent contracting arrangements such as those described above, pressuring for overtime by management personnel, taking pay away from supervisors by not acknowledging overtime, and so on. All of this has had a very disrupting effect, and it is only natural that the interface tensions, which have not been managed, are now appearing in many indirect and disguised ways.

Another angle on this is that Taylor was described by Robertson as having said, "Look, you and I should get together for lunch on a weekly basis ... ." The interpretation I placed on this is that they had not arranged for anything approaching systematic communication between themselves as relates to points of friction between the two plants. Here is a case where needed coordination is not forthcoming by virtue of the absence of a shared basis of understanding. This is a classic Phase 3 interface conflict.

By 11:00 the tensions had dissipated quite a bit. It became apparent that the YXO plant was the intended target since they had negotiated with the independent contractor and they would have to face the consequences of disregarding this danger signal. The pickets had inappropriately located themselves at the wrong gate!

I then sought to resume the interviews. Joe Perkins and I decided to go out to lunch. This necessitated crossing the picket line and provided an interesting study of a new dynamic.

Crossing the Picket Line on the Way Out

As we drove toward the perimeter of the plant and through the security gates, Joe got out to ask the guard whether there was any militancy at the gate. The answer was, "No, not really. They are definitely not happy campers but nothing flagrant has happened." We then drove toward the exit, and Joe turned to me and said, "You had better lock your door," as he locked his own. When we arrived at the picket line, Joe rolled down his window and several of the picketers came toward him. In total violation of Robertson's orders, he said, "What's going on? Nobody in the plant seems to know what's happening. What seems to be the problem?" At this point, Joe concluded that the pickets didn't know what was going on either. Some thought it was related to construction, but Joe pointed out to them that there had been no construction for well over a year. During this interchange, I sat quietly and ventured no information.

From a critique point of view, I thought to myself that it was a serious breakdown to have a second-level manager telling members of the picket line of management's ignorance. I was shocked, and it led me to question the extent to which Joe and possibly others felt any kind of shared membership in the top team.

Interpretation

Later in the week, I arranged for a get-together with the top team to conduct an intensive longitudinal critique and evaluation of this event. Tensions associated with the crisis remained high.

By way of introduction, I introduced the Grid and asked the attendees, who had been joined by Taylor and Walker from the YXO plant, to characterize the kinds of leadership reflected in the top team's performance on Tuesday—the "Picket Line Crisis Day." They had no difficulty in saying, "Robertson, you handled that situation out of the 9,1 corner, didn't you?" This created some tension as that level of openness was uncommon. Robertson said, "You're damn right I did. I've been working out of the 9,1 corner ever since I've been here. That's why we didn't have a wage adjustment this year. That's why we're beginning to see the light at the end of the tunnel." Someone then pointed out, "Not only were you operating in a 9,1 way, you were running a one-man show from your command post. You used us as information-runners, but you did nothing by way of getting input from us as to options or alternatives for grappling with the situation in a more constructive and fundamental way." (Remember the feedback captains received in the cockpit experiments?)

The discussion went on to generalize beyond the Tuesday morning episode. The point was made, "You have used us like slaves for the last eighteen months, and there has to be an end to this road or the party will soon be over. We can't take it and the loss of good people has already become striking. The longer you manage in this way, the greater the likelihood that the better people will leave and then you will only have the dregs to deal with in the future." Robertson again became defensive and said, "What are the alternatives? It seems to me that you've had a good solid eighteen months to begin to take responsibility on your own initiatives, and it still hasn't happened. I have to be the brain who supplies the ideas and who tells you what to do with them."

"That may be true," someone indicated, "but maybe not when viewed from another perspective. We are not uncreative, unthinking people, incapable of dealing with you to handle these problems, but we have never been given the opportunity. You cut the conversation off and, as a result, advocacy is low. We tuck tail rather than tell the truth. Inquiry is nonexistent—we just don't go out looking for problems. So now we're paying the price for failure to develop ourselves as a team."

This provided an occasion for me to describe how the Grid is a useful conceptual schema for seeing actions and options and how it can be used in a deep and comprehensive way for team building to strengthen the use of human resources up and down the organization chain. This brief discussion provoked much interest.

I said, "What else was going on in that session this morning?" People stumbled around but the concentration on Robertson and the top team problem had been so intense that it had dwarfed other possible points. It seemed to me that nothing further was forthcoming, and so I took the occasion to expand the discussion. I turned to Taylor and said, "Joe, what was going on from your point of view?" He replied, "I've been giving very deep thought to that. I realize that we have some emerging troubles that all of us hoped would not appear. It's obvious that a mutual recrimination process is taking place with YXO people trying to put the blame on WFE. Every one of us made the assumption that the picket line, whatever its cause, was not a problem that involved us. Therefore we assumed it was brought about by the tense and negative situation in WFE. That's just how we interpreted it. I have to admit that we were wrong in this diagnosis. We should have correctly identified the problem and borne our responsibility for it as we are the primary contractors for the housekeeping services that are under complaint."

A lively discussion ensued in which the news release (which had been prepared "just in case") was taken apart as a particularly good example. People began to generalize to other points of tension between the two plants. They pointed out that needed cooperation was nonexistent and coordination lacking. It was noted that many opportunities with major bottom-line implications were present for increased interdependence between the two plants but were not being utilized.

I was now able to refocus this two-plant relationship in terms of intergroup conflict and briefly to characterize our way of going about Intergroup Conflict-Solving. We talked about who the attendees would be in such a session. It was explained that they should be the key decision makers plus additional representatives from lower ranks who had resources to contribute in terms of background, particularly in the daily dealing with unions.

Someone then brought up an interesting point and one that highlights the values of such an in situ diagnostic session. The human resource manager said, "I wonder if we could use the Grid as a joint project, treating the two plants as a single entity?" This idea drew much interest. Soon discussion turned to where the seminars might be conducted and when they might be started. Of course, this was preliminary to any firm decision making that would come later.

Critique of In Situ Diagnosis

This situation offers a good example of how a "live" problem can be used diagnostically to identify organization development needs and possible applications for strengthening corporate culture. The unique value of in situ diagnosis is that the evidence of live events is difficult to deny. Close observation during the episode itself and reconstruction with the top team as soon as possible thereafter is much like being able to study a videotape of the event. Reconstruction is more than sufficient for helping the organization to see itself and its *modus operandi* and to consider steps essential for bringing a stronger organization culture into being. It is even better when the in situ event can be placed in the context of interview findings, as was possible in this case. However, the interview findings were not completely accurate because I was not yet aware of the intergroup problem based on reports received from WFE. I feel certain I would have heard about the problem had I started in YXO, but I did not hear about it from WFE. This shows that people report only what seems to be important from their point of view, rather than making systematic observations from a broader corporate framework. The "absence" of a relationship is taken to be the "absence" of problems, which, of course, in this case was not a legitimate conclusion.

Simulations

When a significant problem is known to exist but there are different interpretations of its causes, direct observation of how the problem is being handled might yield a deeper understanding that could resolve the impasse. A diagnostic simulation is an enactment or reenactment of a problem known to exist and to be of importance.

Simulation is a close kin to role play but can be distinguished in the following manner. Role play is defined by procedural action; it virtually communicates a way of seeing the problem at a different level. Simulation also allows us to see a problem more clearly, but its unique feature is the construction of an episode, usually in advance of its actually taking place. Simulation is a replication to test phenomenological validity.

Since we use both techniques in our organization development efforts, a further distinction may be useful. Role play as well as psychodrama motivate by helping the role player or participant to gain a better understanding of the problem being enacted. Simulation, on the other hand, has historically meant to dry-run a problem so that the investigator can comprehend more fundamentally the underlying dynamics of the particular situation. Participants may learn during the process, but this is incidental to the primary purpose except when used in a training context. In this sense, simulation is a test of the model. That is, it is not the blueprint of a wind tunnel, but rather a drawn-to-scale mock-up of how the blueprinted wind tunnel can be expected to operate under specified conditions.

The distinctions we have made are not hard and fast. Many illustrations suggest that the terms are used interchangeably. For example, consider the illustration of crew members in the modern jet cockpit from Chapter 1. These pilots, as well as all other commercial airline pilots, are required by Federal Aviation Administration standards to undergo annual recurrent training. For the United pilots, this involves working through a flight scenario in a simulator, the purpose being to learn how better to grapple with problems that are difficult to anticipate during actual flight. In this case, the learner is not the investigator; the learner is the pilot. However, this use of the word simulation is probably the exception rather than the rule.

In the cockpit example, we did engage in a simulation activity in order to determine the true nature of a problem. We began the process with an interview-based diagnostic approach, which led to the conclusion that erosion of captain authority and crew discipline was the causal factor of diminished crew effectiveness. However, we were reluctant to accept the conclusion that strengthening captain authority per se was a solution. Therefore we decided to test the initial conclusions through diagnostic simulation. This allowed us to experience directly how captains usually exercised authority in the cockpit setting. It provided an opportunity to deepen our understanding of the dynamics present within the cockpit and to arrive at an independent diagnosis of the problem.

The pilots in simulated crews enacted the problem solving by showing how they would resolve a safety dilemma while "flying" a leg, say, from Los Angeles to New York. In the majority of cases, those who were portraying "captains" took the lead in such a way as to exclude input from those in first or second officer roles. Rather than insubordination on the part of lower level roles, the reaction was blind compliance. At the end of each simulation, crew members critiqued their performance in the presence of one another and with the designers. Those in subordinate roles let it be known that their solutions had neither been heard nor requested. It seemed not to be a problem of respect for captain authority, but something quite different.

Critique of the simulations along with our observations of what was going on led to a more general discussion in which we asked the crews, "What is the real problem? Is it one of strengthening the exercise of captain authority and discipline? If not, then what is it?" The crews concluded that the problem preventing the full mobilization of resources is the captain centralizing authority, thereby shutting out available input from other crew members.

This example also demonstrates a situation in which initial interview findings proved contradictory to conclusions reached from simulations. This points out the limitation of excessive reliance on interviewing. Furthermore, since the captains themselves had reached the conclusion, resistance to change was automatically eliminated. In other words, it wasn't a matter of consultants drawing conclusions and telling them what to do. Rather, those who own the problem reached conclusions that consultants were in a position to reinforce. This is what we call a "self-convincing" experience.

Simulations have proven useful in clarifying and deepening understanding of many other problems of diagnosis. For example, when managers tell us that union officers are militant, we ask, "Why?" The answer frequently is, "That's all they know," or "They're out to get reelected." So sometimes we have these same managers take the role of union officers who then attempt to enact a typical contract clause. The formality of discussion, the lack of openness and candor, and the win/lose mentality quickly come into focus and participants become aware of the deeper nature of corporate culture. The problem is found to lie in union/management relations rather than being an intrinsic characteristic of one group or the other. Then, the design of an intervention to restore mutual respect can be implemented, based on a sounder concept of the problem to be solved, in this case, an intergroup conflict problem.

Here is an example drawn from the union/management negotiations area.

A radical proposal had been under consideration for some time, and it seemed critical to gain some insight into what the union's initial reactions might be.

A group of first- and second-level supervisors and managers was assigned union officer roles and provided background information on typical union reactions to management proposals. Without being able to anticipate the particular proposal about to be introduced, they met with the formally designated management bargaining committee and the radical proposal was put on the table. They reacted by immediately calling a caucus within which they explored their personal reactions and feelings as well as probing the deeper implications of the proposal for the future of the union and its members. Their reactions were affirmative.

The end result was that, on returning to the bargaining table, those portraying union members rejected the proposal out of hand and provided numerous reasons to explain its unacceptability.

At this point the simulation was terminated, and management was given an opportunity to inquire of those who had portrayed union members why the proposal had been rejected. The conclusion was self-evident. They had rejected the proposal based on the unilateral "take-it-or-leave-it" attitude with which management had presented it, having felt offended and treated as though unworthy of respectful treatment. Those who had portrayed union members went on to explain that initially their reaction to the proposal had been quite positive and favorable.

This trial run gave management insight into its critical error of approach as well as the ideological soundness of the proposal per se. This served as the basis for renewed efforts at actual bargaining.

In this simulation, management constituted the learning group. The supervisors and managers who portrayed union officers, though they gained insights into being union representatives through the experience, acquired such insights as an incidental part of the greater purpose of the simulation.

Here is another illustration.

Training in dynamic management had been underway for some time, but resistances to implementation were being encountered among wage personnel. The question arose, "Would it be feasible to engage wage people in studying managerial concepts?" Or, "Would these concepts be difficult for them to understand since they had not had managerial experience?"

To answer this question, a prototype of management training essentially identical in concept and detail, save for use of managerial language, i.e., boss, subordinate, colleague, and so on, was designed. A random sample of wage people was invited to take part in this evaluative learning. They accepted. Tests and questions as completed at the end of this prototype demonstrated a level of comprehension comparable to that achieved by management. Data also confirmed a high degree of enthusiasm for this kind of learning among wage personnel.

In this case, wage personnel had learned concrete problem-solving skills of direct use to them. Nevertheless the main purpose of the activity was the evaluation of the feasibility of this kind of training and development effort implemented in the wage ranks.

A final example involves a role play, the feasibility of which was first tested through the use of simulation. A client company solicited our services to help them institute a systematic approach to goal setting that would tie into a steepened incentive reward curve. We began this process through a series of twenty-two interviews and then recruited a task force of three organization members to act as resources in the development of a test design.

In preparation for the seminar, we had two members of the task force extemporaneously dry-run our proposed goal-setting sequence. In this way we were able to assess the viability of this strategy. In the pilot seminar composed of twenty-six participants, we had boss/subordinate pairs role play the goal-setting sequence. These were true boss/subordinate groupings, each dealing with actual goals to be set in place for the subordinate in the upcoming year.

We indicated that this was a working seminar; in other words, a secondary purpose to their own learning involved our testing the validity of the design for their situation.

The general reaction was that it proved to be an eye-opening experience, and the approach was validated from our own standpoint as well. Rather than seek to implement a mechanical approach as had characterized their past efforts, they discovered new insights by using a "dynamic" approach to deal with the "mechanics" of the situation.

The same has been done in terms of reenacting disputes about capital appropriations, making up the budget, and bringing issues of product quality into bold relief. Simulating a problem has deepened understanding of underlying dynamics and served to strengthen convictions that the problem merits further attention. When these kinds of specific problems are seen as particular episodes, organization members quickly realize that unhealthy corporate culture is a significant problem toward which effort must be directed in order to achieve greater corporate effectiveness.

Participant Observation

A fourth major way of organization diagnosis, and in many respects the soundest of the four, is through participant observation. As mentioned earlier, participant observation is a tool par excellence used by anthropologists to study other cultures. The anthropologist gains entrance into some significant component of the culture and engages in a physical "live-in." The period may be a month or a year, and it may be repeated on a routine basis, perhaps annually.

This diagnostic methodology is probably the least disruptive, particularly after the first few days. People become accustomed to the consultant's presence much as a piece of furniture comes to be accepted, and therefore little note is made of it. This awareness depends to a large extent on the consultant's body language, and can be influenced by whether or not the consultant talks "out of school."

The purpose of participant observation is to understand how the culture works and in every way possible avoid actions that might focus the attention of those who are its carriers toward self-examination. The goal is not to help people change the culture, but only to understand it. A careful anthropologist maintains a diary, uses cameras, and keeps very detailed notes regarding observations.

Later the distinctive and unique features of that culture can be characterized and reported.

Participant observation may make use of all three of the previously discussed diagnostic approaches, but it is more encompassing. Interviews may reveal how participants in the organization view it, each from his or her own perspective. In situ diagnosis may shed new light on critical incidents. Simulations may foster further understanding of subtle problems that resist easy interpretation.

Participant observation used in organization development work may extend over a two-month period, or even longer, depending on the particular circumstance, the organization complexity, and the depth of study thought to be important. An illustration of a typical participant observation start-up is provided from dictation taken at the time in which the event occurred. It highlights some of the considerations that merit understanding in evaluating this approach.

> Quinn Morton, the key executive at Lakeside, went to a Grid Seminar where I was one of the seminar managers. I didn't get to know him personally at the time but, because I took some responsibility for lectures and critique periods during general sessions, he got to know something of my thinking. The last Thursday after dinner, he and I began talking about the week's learning. He said he was impressed with some of the issues we had focused on because they represented the kinds of dilemmas he was trying to deal with day after day at Lakeside.
>
> As we continued talking, an idea began to take shape. He finally put it into words, "Look, Bob, would you be interested in coming to Lakeside for two or three months to help us learn how to put these principles into practice and thereby increase our effectiveness as an organization? Our goal would be to see how good you can make a company when you really go all out to make it excellent." That was the kind of challenge that doesn't come along every day. After some deliberation, I agreed to do so and the Lakeside project came into being. Three phases of organization development (Grid OD) were involved.
>
> In Phase 1, several hundred managerial personnel attended seminars to learn Grid theories regarding individual, group,

and intergroup factors influencing action and problem solving. The idea was that before people could really think constructively in terms of organization excellence, they needed to examine and understand fundamental issues of conflict, teamwork, openness, candor, and so on.

The next step was for me to move physically into the company with the task of getting the principles that had been learned applied to the operational problem-solving life of Lakeside. For about two months I did an initial study of the organization and interviewed many of the people I'd gotten to know in the seminars.

From the outset, I had specified the conditions under which I would join the organization. It was agreed that if I joined, I would in no way involve myself in personnel evaluation. I wanted no part in trying to influence reconstruction of the power system in terms of "which people should be placed in what roles," though I did have great interest in helping the organization membership reconstruct its own power system. I had clear reason for adopting this approach. It was that, to a substantial degree, the problems of an organization are not to be found "inside" people but are more closely related to organization-wide assumptions as to how people should relate to one another and to attitudes existing between groups. Therefore my contribution would be to help people directly in their relations with one another, to help reform interpersonal attitudes within teams, which constituted Phase 2, and to help resolve problems between groups (Phase 3).

These are the first three phases of Grid OD. It was also made clear that if it turned out to be necessary or desirable, we might also look at the next two phases of Grid OD—Ideal Strategic Corporate Modeling (Phase 4) and its Implementation (Phase 5).

From the outset, I made it clear that I wanted no company membership, that is, no car, no office, no telephone number, or any other symbol that might imply I was occupying a position within Lakeside's organizational format. This point is extremely important when the diagnostic strategy is based on participant observation. One reason is that an outsider such as myself has little difficulty gaining access to lower ranks of the organization. However, if the consultant positions him or herself at some location midway up the organization hierarchy, he or she has much greater difficulty in dealing openly and in a collegiate sense with people above or below the set rank. Another reason is that, generally speaking, people are eager to know who you're reporting to and what you may be saying and doing. If it is known that you have no direct reporting relationship but rather are responsible to the organization for assisting it with effectiveness, you have much more credibility and far greater access to the secrets of the organization that might not otherwise come your way.

I joined the organization under these conditions. For some time, initially, it was difficult for Quinn to adjust to my presence without forever asking me with whom I was working and on what problems I was "engaged." Frequently, he quizzed me on these points, but on each occasion I referred him to our earlier agreement. I told him that I appreciated his need to monitor my performance, but on the other hand he needed to appreciate my problem of ensuring that the confidences and secrets presently being entrusted to me would continue to be made available. This would be the case only if I maintained the conditions of nonreporting we had previously agreed upon. I did tell him that he was under no constraint from probing his own line organization to find out what I was doing and what their reactions to it were. He came to accept this.

During this initial period, I avoided as much as possible spending my time on chance contacts and sought to implement a broad design that I had previously thought through. I attached myself to the top team. It consisted of fourteen members and met frequently, sometimes on a planned schedule and equally as often on an unplanned basis. At the first session, Quinn introduced me, though I already knew several of the members, and from that time on they quickly became accustomed to my silent presence. For two months I listened and took notes but talked with no one about what I was learning. During this period, however, I developed strong convictions about many of the deeper organization problems that literally had to be brought into focus for this organization to escape its own history.

Quinn was a quizzer. He quizzed everybody, almost one after another, for the minutest detail of what was happening in the various departments and functions. I thought this was more or less like cross-examination, but I didn't attach seriousness to it until later.

I also made it a point to attend the meetings conducted by the various members of the top team in their own settings. There were too many of these to attend every one, but I was able to attend enough to look for common threads.

Almost every top-team member held a stand-up, or what they called a "touch-base," meeting immediately prior to any top-team meeting. This was for the purpose of loading each member with the latest information so that when quizzed by Quinn, the individual would be able to provide solid data and not get "caught." Although people respected Quinn, they resented this aspect of his leadership and thought it wasteful of his time and theirs. They also resented spending so much effort on trivial detail because it deprived the top team of looking more closely at the big picture. Since I have seen this leadership style many times, I drew the conclusion that it represented a central issue that should be confronted as time went on. So a natural first step to application was to conduct team-building sessions with Quinn and his team. This was the number one power and authority problem in that organization. Quinn had always thought about it in the sense of keeping people on their toes, but he unwittingly forfeited their input on corporate vision.

In any event, during the intervention phase of the organization development work, the team-building sessions led to a critical formulation. This was that team members would no longer feel obligated to feed Quinn every last detail, even though he queried for such information. Rather, Quinn would delegate responsibility to department heads for conducting their department and functional affairs in a sound way. This performance would be reviewed on a quarterly basis. Numerous other conclusions were reached but, as a result of this one decision, a date was set in April for each of the department and staff heads to have worked through with his or her own team the increased responsibility that they were about to shoulder for running their organizations effectively.

By April, this delegation was essentially complete. It had a very invigorating effect on the top team and released energies among them that permitted entry into a Phase 4 activity, i.e., redesigning the corporation to align it to the soundest principles of management and organization that people were capable of implementing.

During the participant observation period (prior to intervention), I also learned much of the deep and long-lasting conflict between the operations department and the maintenance people. Maintenance was controlled by a union contract that prevented operations personnel from making even minor adjustments that had not previously been written into job descriptions. All modifications had to be made by the maintenance organization. As a result, maintenance was overburdened by minor operations requirements. Maintenance had the power to place in priority of importance work orders for overall effectiveness of operations, not just provide service on a first-come, first-served basis. Therefore, the quality of the relationship was more or less in the control of the maintenance people with the operations personnel at their mercy. All of this, I concluded, had to be worked out as one of the major intergroup activities of that organization.

Two other issues need to be mentioned. One was an intergroup friction of serious proportions between the departments and headquarters. The concern was that they were falling behind competition, leading to loss of market share. This was used by headquarters to pressure departments for greater productivity and was deeply resented. So this also became a potential candidate for Phase 3 intervention. Finally, the union/management problems had reached serious proportions with the union using grievances as a way of tying up management and management setting conferences with union leadership late in the day so as to inconvenience union officers during the last hour of work.

Ideal Strategic Corporate Modeling and Phase 5 Implementation critically influenced the success of this organization. The general terms of the model involved studying existing facilities and equipment, with the conclusion that whenever a new operational unit was brought on stream, it would be grafted onto one of the existing ones. The whole physical infrastructure, therefore, that had been put in place at the beginning was approaching its limits. It was decided that because there were seven hundred acres, only fifty of which were being used, a grand design should be created for how to use this entire acreage most productively. An infrastructure was established that enabled many new additions that would otherwise have been located at other sites. Elevation in their competitive standing followed as a direct result of this reordering action.

In any event, at the end of my two month tenure at Lakeside, I requested an all-day meeting with the top team and provided a detailed diagnosis of what had been learned during the eight-week period and with proposed next steps, all of which were successfully implemented over the next two years.

Comparison of the Four Human Resource Diagnostic Approaches

As mentioned earlier, there probably is no one best way of organization diagnosis. The soundest approach may be all of them in varying combinations. Interviews are generally a good first step in developing an orientation to what needs to be examined in greater depth. A potential problem to keep in mind is that organization members often seek to put their best foot forward so as to present their company in a favorable light. This may be intentional or not, but in some cases people tend to draw together and paint a rosy picture in an interview situation. Thus the consultant must observe the deeper underlying dynamics present in the situation.

In situ diagnosis has the advantage of providing what may be a more accurate view of what is really going on in an organization because it portrays the unfolding of an event as it is actually happening. People are caught up in the action, and as a result the true dynamics of the interaction often appear in bold relief. When confronted with facts that they themselves have just experienced, reality is difficult to deny and self-deception is thereby removed. This sets the stage for the beginning of change.

Simulations offer much the same in that they replicate a situation that brings to the forefront the real-life handling of problems. They offer a self-convincing experience where people come face to face with how they actually relate to others in accomplishing a particular task. Feedback and critique serve to illuminate options that could enhance effectiveness in getting the job done.

Information obtained from both in situ diagnosis and simulations can serve to validate or invalidate conclusions from other approaches. Participant observation is probably the strongest because it puts organization development into the organization under semi-natural conditions, with freedom of access over time to any portion of the organization and without responsibility for achieving quick and demonstrable results. The consultant can interview, rely on simulations, follow up on in situ happenings, and come to a significantly deeper understanding than might be possible by any method employed in isolation.

Other Approaches

There are several other approaches to organization diagnosis beyond those described here. They deserve mention and are supplemental to the primary sources just outlined. These sources include survey research, sociotechnical analysis, and others, which are often conducted by the human resource department of the company concerned. When these well-known approaches are already being employed by a company, we prefer not to repeat them. Readministration of questionnaires and response forms tends to become boring and repetitious, although it may not necessarily reduce their validity. One variation on questionnaires and response forms that we have found useful is presented elsewhere.[1]

Beyond surveys and questionnaires, we also employ numerous public sources to provide useful diagnostic information. For example, *The Wall Street Journal* contains up-to-date reporting on major organizational developments. It provides a good picture of changing arrangements in terms of mergers and acquisitions, bankruptcies, hirings, firings, miscues, and the difficulties being encountered as well as stories of exemplary performances. By virtue of having worked with many of the companies cited, we are often able to read between the lines, filling in the underlying dynamics in these situations. These findings can be generalized and patterns further established. Much the same can be said about such periodicals as *Fortune, Forbes, Business Week,* and others aimed at more specialized business disciplines. *Inc.* is a useful source of case studies that entail the successful handling of some important situations and the underlying rationale. Keeping up to date in this way forces us to maintain a broad orientation and keeps us informed on developing trends in both global and American business and industry.

Summary

This chapter illustrates several effective ways of behavioral culture diagnosis. The importance of valid diagnosis to the success of an organization development effort cannot be overemphasized. When organization development work is limited to providing help on nuts-and-bolts problem solving or simply conducting seminars on time or stress management and quality circles, at best only incremental improvement can be anticipated. This is not the kind of big change so essential for strengthening corporate competitiveness. Rather, it is the kind of piecemeal change that diverts attention from the bigger picture.

With a comprehensive orientation and sound diagnostic work, it becomes possible to confront a company's top team with the outstanding problems residing within their own culture and to stimulate the kind of motivation essential for inducing major organization change.

Reference

1. Blake, R. R., and J. S. Mouton. 1972. *How to Assess the Strengths and Weaknesses of a Business Enterprise.* Austin: Scientific Methods, Inc.

5

Learning About Behavior Dynamics

A way to understand Grid Organization Development (Grid OD) is to describe the various kinds of activities involved. Presume that your organization has been moving along an evolutionary path. As vice president of marketing, you feel profitability is acceptable but not exemplary. Market share has been retained but has not increased markedly. New products emerge from time to time, more or less geared to maintaining an equilibrium as older products complete their life cycles. It is a good company. Ethics in dealing with customers and suppliers are sound, and people are well treated. Salaries and wages compare favorably with area competition as do fringe benefits. Those who join the company, like yourself, think of themselves as building their careers with it. You know, however, that the margin between the company's performance as it actually is and what it could become is substantial. You have an uneasy feeling that more verve and vitality could be applied to solving some of the company's problems.

Getting Acquainted with Grid Ideas

How does a company go about laying the groundwork for behavioral excellence? Suppose you have decided to launch an OD effort in your organization. How exactly do you get started?

Perhaps the first step to consider is how to develop a first-hand understanding of the Grid properties of 9,9 management. Although you could sit down and read a book, the best understanding comes from direct experience. This can be accomplished by attending a Grid Seminar designed to increase understanding of basic principles of 9,9 management and to provide each participant with insight into his or her own personal style of managing.

Before coming to the seminar, you are asked to study a book about the Grid[1,2] and to complete a series of measurement instruments characterizing yourself, your team, and your organization. This preparatory work is designed to help you evaluate your understanding of the basic concepts presented in the text. Time for completion of this work varies with reading ability of the participant. Generally it takes about twenty hours.

The first activity is a general session in which the learning objectives are described. These include

1. Personal or self-learning,
2. Learning about problem solving in teams,
3. Learning about managing intergroup conflict, and
4. Learning about how to achieve an excellent organization culture.

Following this introduction, the first team project begins. Imagine yourself as a member of one of several teams. In a public seminar, members of your team are drawn from companies other than your own. When staged on an in-house basis, team composition is based on achieving a good mix of different positions and levels, with no boss and subordinate pairing occurring within the same team.

Your team has the same problem to solve as the other teams and in the same amount of time. All teams are challenged to achieve a high-quality result. The problems and projects throughout the week, like the first one, are measured quantitatively to evaluate how good a job your team was able to do in getting a sound result. Your team does not have an appointed leader, any prescribed procedures, or a facilitator. How effectively the team works in solving the problem at hand rests on the team itself. Upon completion of the problem-solving activity, each team returns to the general session room where scoring provides the raw material for each team to evaluate its own effectiveness. Scores are posted to indicate how effectively each team worked to develop a solution.

Then each team returns to its meeting place for the purpose of examining how it worked in achieving its result. During these critique periods, you and the other members of your team investigate what occurred as you tried to solve the problem. The critique periods in a Grid are often the most stimulating points in a seminar. They provide the basis for examining and thoroughly understanding what differentiates a good, high-powered, results-oriented, problem-solving team from a poor or ineffective one. The team also examines what each member did or did not do and the extent to which each person contributed to the team achievement as a whole. Individual member Grid styles are discussed in terms of impact on task results.

There are several projects of this kind. The content of each is different, but the tasks focus on one facet or another of what constitutes effective operation. By solving the problems presented, team members are in fact exploring the substance of the Grid more deeply and by inquiring into how the team operates, members are able to formulate a model of excellent teamwork and high performance standards. They are then able to compare this model with less effective problem-solving approaches.

Another activity involves interaction between representatives of two different teams meeting in pairs to compare performance on prepared formulations that have been created within the teams and that characterize the properties of managerial effectiveness. In this way each pair member serves his or her team as a negotiating representative to bring into view the many aspects of behavioral dynamics related to win/lose attitudes present in everyday organization life. Many parallels can be drawn back to an on-the-job application relating to conflict situations such as those between management and the union, between marketing and manufacturing, between programmers and end users, or any two groups representing a wide range of win/lose antagonism, compromise, or bargaining.

Another kind of insight gained from the Grid is more personal. This concerns learning about yourself as a manager and how you relate to others who may manage in ways different from your own. How exactly does this occur? As points of disagreement appear or as impasses occur in solving team problems, team members respond in their characteristic ways, each revealing various degrees of initiative, inquiry, advocacy (expressing opinions), conflict resolution, decision making, and critique. When five or six people are involved in this kind of an intense learning activity, they gain considerable insight into one another's leadership style. This knowledge enables them to engage in an activity toward the end of the seminar that is at the very heart of personal effectiveness learning.

Using the Grid framework as the foundation, your team members write a descriptive paragraph on how they have seen you operate during the course of the week. The person being described is often asked to write the paragraph as it is being formulated onto a flipchart pad, but this individual is not to offer any input at this point. We have found that the best learning occurs during this activity when the person being focused on just listens to what is being said. Any defensiveness, whether perceived or real, tends to stifle candor and spontaneity on the part of team members and therefore may not contribute to maximum learning. Upon completion, the individual then has the opportunity to probe others for the reasons underlying what they have said and to receive constructive feedback regarding how future interaction skills can be improved and made more effective. What you actually receive from other team members is an outside view of yourself that you can take to compare with your own inside view and use accordingly in efforts toward personal change.

Each member of the team receives such a written description. Many managers agree that it is a highly valuable lesson in gaining objectivity and in reducing self-deception. For many it is the beginning of real change, for it affords a person a way of seeing how he or she is operating and comparing it with the 9,9 model of managerial excellence. A few managers conclude at the end of this activity that the way they operated prior to the seminar is already very close to the 9,9 style, but most find a wide gap between the ways in which they have operated previously and the manner they realized would be more sound were they able to accomplish it. Although 67.9 percent describe themselves as 9,9 prior to the Grid experience, upon conclusion of the program in a post self-assessment, this number has dwindled to 16.5 percent.[3] We call this the "stripping away of self-deception." Becoming more objective about oneself is the first big step toward change.

This gap-producing experience of Grid Organization Development is significant for most people in a company. It is an eye-opener as many managers, following a Grid Seminar, find themselves strongly committed to doing what is necessary to change for the better.

Toward the end of the seminar, you participate in an activity that involves studying organization culture as it exists within your company. This puts you in an excellent position to examine the gap between the dominant mode of the behavior culture in your company and the 9,9 model of excellence. Most managers find this a very rewarding, though sometimes disquieting, experience. It brings them face to face with the magnitude and depth of the problems that constitute barriers to excellence.

The whole learning situation is based on a self-convincing approach. It is a process of self-discovery, self-testing, self-comparison, self-judgment, and self-evaluation. Only you can draw conclusions as to the meaning of what you have learned for yourself and its implications for your leadership in the organization.

Gaining Commitment to Next Steps

The true impact of the learning experience can be seen once you return to the job. When you walk in on Monday, ask what has happened and listen to the problems. You will be impressed by the Grid styles you see operating in your boss, colleagues, and subordinates, as well as by your own responses to them. This direct evidence of how the firm is being managed opens up new gaps never before apparent to you. You and others who have attended Grid Seminars will probably be putting your heads together to see how it all adds up. Many report that after four to six weeks of reflection, they find themselves planning how to implement further steps of development.

Remember the cockpit example from Chapter 1 where the captains attended a Grid Seminar and then came back to the line. They had new convictions ("two o'clock norms") about how to achieve greater effectiveness and safety in the cockpit. However, their team members, the first and second officers, were still operating according to the old culture ("ten o'clock norms"). When captains sought more open interaction and two-way communication in the cockpit, the other two cockpit crew members perceived this as uncertainty and lack of leadership. How, then, does one go back to the job and seek to do things differently given the culture already set in place?

Suppose you are at this point and have developed "two o'clock" convictions, whereas those around you (boss, colleagues, or subordinates) are still operating according to "ten o'clock" convictions. Several steps may suggest themselves to you. An important one is to invite other managers to attend a Grid Seminar to see if their conclusions, when they return, match your own. Perhaps five or six others might attend a Grid Seminar voluntarily. A description of such a situation follows.

The other vice-presidents in my company had already been to a Managerial Grid Seminar, so by the time I boarded the plane to attend, I had heard repeatedly that I was in for quite an experience. Our president was sending all key managers to public seminars, and now it was my turn to go. My friends made a few jokes as they speculated about the kind of personal "feedback" I might receive from others on my seminar team. I wasn't quite sure what they were talking about and felt a little uneasy about finding out.

I had read the *Managerial Grid* book as part of my prework, so I had some idea about the content of the seminar. I knew my own Grid style, or so I thought. Later I learned that the *experience* of team membership during the seminar activities gave me far more insight into my managerial style than years of book learning could ever have provided.

As I checked into the hotel, I wondered what the other managers would be like, especially since I knew we would be working together in teams. Several days seemed like such a long time to go over some management principles. There was so much work to do back at the office ...

When we met in the dining room, I was pleased to find sales managers, marketing directors, personnel vice presidents, and other operating managers from business and government organizations. Everyone seemed just as curious as I was about the Grid Seminar we had come to.

Right away we were assigned to teams. There were five other managers on mine, the Blue Team. After a brief orientation session, we were directed to our team rooms to work on the first task. Our assignment as a team was to come up with the best answers we could on the same written test that we had done individually before coming to the seminar.

We thought our answers were pretty good. Some of us felt fairly confident and persuaded the others to go along with us. Other times, we voted on the best answer. We felt very pleased with our final team result. However, after we got back to general session for scoring of individual and team answers, we were in for a rude shock. Those of us who had been so sure of ourselves turned out to have the lowest scores and had led the team astray. The quietest person on our team actually scored higher than the team score. Something was definitely wrong with our team interaction, and we began to realize that we had a long way to go before we reached team synergy. The dynamics of synergy made sense to us—that through the combined efforts of all its members, the team's results could be of higher quality than those of any of its individual members. This was our objective.

We also learned about critique—a systematic review of our performance and planning for more effective approaches. This was a big departure from the way most of us worked. For example, my usual style had been to try to avoid commenting on other people's work until I got fed up, and then I really let them have it. This ongoing critique at all stages of an activity seemed to be much more productive for keeping us on course with our goal. It really made us stop, think, and recast our strategy a little bit. With each team activity, we became more and more adept at using critique skills to the team's advantage. Our synergy increased dramatically, and it became measurably evident in our team effectiveness ratings.

On the second or third day of the seminar I noticed that I was becoming more conscious of my own behavior as I participated in team discussions. Since we had been using so much critique and knew the criteria for good teamwork, I could often tell when I was getting off track and I'd try to reorient my behavior.

Probably the most powerful aspect of the seminar was the fact that we actually experienced the principles of teamwork. There was very little passive learning of the type that is standard with most training I've been in. We were active the whole week, from the first thing in the morning until 9 or 10 at night. The week really went by fast because we were always *learning by doing.*

The tasks were structured so I didn't experience the frustration I've sometimes felt when we just sat around in discussion groups and talked about someone's feelings. Instead, each time we met, there were clear instructions and a deadline to meet. Tensions and problems that came out in the course of our activities could all be addressed in terms of our tasks rather than as personal criticism. For instance, when one of our team members thought I was dominating a discussion we were having, he reminded me that we needed to hear from those who had made useful points earlier. For the sake of our team results, we needed more input than was being offered by my worn-out argument.

One of the most beneficial insights I received was during the personal feedback session toward the end of the week. We took turns describing one another's behavior. Because we had performed so many team tasks during the week, we had been given the opportunity to observe each person's work behavior in a fair amount of depth. Since we had been working at achieving candor during team critiques, the feedback session came as a natural climax to the whole process. My teammates wrote down various adjectives to describe me and then used them to compose a paragraph that offered suggestions as to how I could constructively change my behavior. A few of the adjectives they used to describe me were humorous; some were contradictory; but most of them seemed to be uncannily accurate observations.

Since most of the other managers I work with have also attended a Grid, they have been able to reinforce the feedback I received at the seminar and support the changes I want to make in *how* I reach decisions, manage conflict, and advocate my positions. Under pressure, it was easy sometimes to slip back into my old pattern of seizing complete control over decisions that affect my unit. It has become clear that when I do that, I deprive myself and our unit of some of the best resources we have available. The added advantage of this new participative approach is that others involved in the *process* of solving the problem are much more likely to carry out that solution successfully. We share a new sense of commitment to success.

As indicated earlier in this chapter, after you and the members of your real-life work team have attended a Grid Seminar, you might meet to discuss and evaluate your learning in order to see if additional steps might be taken. If the decision is to proceed, two immediate options present themselves. One is for a group of managers to undertake a field study of different approaches to organization development as a basis for comparing which approach best fits the firm's requirements for moving forward. If the decision is to go with a Grid OD effort, the process of taking the Grid in-house usually proceeds as follows.

First, key people at the top of the organization attend a public Grid. This permits them to understand the theory and gain commitment to its application within the organization. In this "seeding" step, it is generally best if these people are high-level line people since their commitment is often necessary for the needed approval and follow-through to ensure a sound investment in terms of time and money as evidenced at the bottom line.

These same people or others who have attended a Grid Seminar then participate in an Instructor Preparation program. We recommend that at least one of these individuals be a high-level line manager as this demonstrated commitment by upper management to the change effort is more likely to gain the support of lower levels. In contrast to "change by edict," it generates a spirit of "We're all in this together."

The next step is to run a pilot program of about twenty-four people, teamed in such a way that no boss and his or her subordinate are on the same team. This seminar is run by two of the people who have completed Instructor Preparation. Additional instructors for running subsequent programs may also be trained at this time. An effective approach is to continue to rotate line managers into the instructor learning sequence and, as these managers are trained, those who conducted the previous seminars are relieved of their role and can return to organizational duty, passing on the development responsibility to others. In this way, no single line manager is drawn away from his or her own job responsibilities for a prolonged period of time. At the same time, organizational commitment to the OD effort runs high due to widespread line instructor involvement.

Another step that can be taken simultaneously is involvement in an Organization Development Seminar. This seminar provides several organization members with a more comprehensive, hands-on or "how to do it" feeling for applying the strategies and tactics of development as illustrated in this book but for specific implementation in their own firms. This should be undertaken by those who will be responsible for the overall change effort. It provides a "big picture" of next steps after Grid seminar attendance, including team building, intergroup conflict resolution, and ideal strategic corporate modeling. In the Organization Development Seminar, these activities are studied through simulations in order for those who attend to gain a comprehensive understanding of the entire sequence of phases and activities that make up the Grid approach to organization development. These will be discussed in more detail in later chapters.

Following these several preparatory steps discussed up to this point, a company is in good shape to make a go/no-go decision as to whether to proceed with further Grid activities. If the decision is made to move forward, Grid training is taken down through all levels of the organization, but even then the training is tailor-made to the particular needs of any specific company.

Summary

By the time Grid learning has been completed throughout the organization, every organization member has had the opportunity to learn:

1. The theories of the Grid as a systematic way of thinking about behavior dynamics,
2. Some of the skills involved in synergistic teamwork,
3. The use of critique to find out *what* is right (rather than *who* is right) and to assess whether or not corrections need to be made, and
4. The contribution that openness and candor can make, both in getting down to the brass-tacks issues that must be faced and in promoting creativity.

At the completion of Grid Seminar training by about half of the corporate membership, the organization has achieved critical mass. Things begin to happen. It is the first significant point in converting to a problem-solving culture. A generalized tension for forward progress appears between the way managers are managing a firm and the way they should be managing it by virtue of the developing awareness among the management ranks of an ideal/ actual discrepancy. Corporate members experience the desire to take the learning and do something concrete with it. This is when pay-out can truly be seen. Projects are defined around problems that have caused persistent difficulties. Managers are assigned to project teams to develop recommendations, solutions, or answers as to what should be done to solve these persistent and perplexing problems. This is a critical time in development. When managers begin to see things happen by closing even some of the gaps, a new sense of urgency emerges. Accomplishment comes from seeing problems solved. This reinforces the readiness to try harder. The spirit of a "can do" attitude provides a clear indication that new energy, up to now tightly locked in, is at last available.

References

1. Blake, R. R., and J. S. Mouton. 1990. *The Managerial Grid IV*. Houston: Gulf Publishing.

2. Blake, R. R. and J. S. Mouton. 1985. *The Managerial Grid III*. Houston: Gulf Publishing.

3. *Ibid*, p. 182.

6

The Beginning of Pay-Out

After people experience basic Grid training of the sort described in Chapter 5, culture-wide issues can be brought more clearly into view through Phase 1A projects. This is where bottom-line results from the training investment made thus far begin to appear.

To recapitulate, by this time many or most organization members have been in a learning seminar and have found the opportunity to work as self-regulating team members to be a new and rewarding experience. Now the potential exists for family teams to engage in the same kind of learning regarding the actual culture prevailing in that team. However, this must be delayed until all members of the family team have attended the basic seminar. Thus an enthusiasm for effort to improve work has been created, but the chance for concrete application has not yet come about.

We can, however, focus on and subject to change one kind of work problem even at this early point in the game. The problems we are talking about are those that belong to no one in particular and yet in another sense they belong to all. These are not problems that are lodged within any one team. Rather, they evolve from the corporate culture itself. They derive from norms that govern the ways in which people interact with one another as they perform work tasks. They are, for example, problems that arise by virtue of not wanting to look bad when compared to one's peers. In other words, it may be known that a certain action is right, but a supervisor may choose instead to ignore the problem on the basis that his or her colleagues are also reluctant to take action. The case study presented in this chapter exemplifies this point. Historically those problems have not been subject to resolution by the exercise of power and authority. Rather, they tend to persist in spite of efforts to solve them. This leads to the notion that a different character of intervention may be needed.

Quality might be thought of as such an overriding problem. Safety is another. Both are normative problems that presume the existence of a shared practice by which people act, almost as a second-nature. When organization members have learned the Grid way of operating, this learning can be brought to bear on changing these kinds of organization-wide norms in order to overcome complacency and to achieve greater levels of effectiveness. However, this requires the employment of special designs for grappling with normative issues that are present beneath the problem itself.

Establishing Sound Norms

As a result of social blindness or exaggerated individualism, managers who want to change behavior often disregard the existence of norms. Norms are the sinews that hold the corporate culture together. Although cultures cannot be seen and changed directly, it is possible to demonstrate the existence of norms.

As illustrated in Chapter 3, a norm is any uniformity of attitude, opinion, feeling, or action shared by two or more people. Any group is characterized by the norms its members share. For all practical purposes, a team could not be a team if it lacked norms that served to regulate and coordinate interactions among members. The reason is that there would be no basis for cooperation.

The concept of norms and other terms related to it (such as traditions, precedents, and past practices) are not often used to talk about individuals. Individuals may be "norms carriers," but the norms belong to the team. On the other hand, concepts such as attitudes, opinions, and feelings convey something about individuals that teams lack. Individuals have opinions; teams do not. All these words describe something viewed from the perspective of the individual.

Bosses more frequently than not disregard or don't "see" norms and rely on the exercise of unilateral power to compel shifts in behavior even when these are resisted. A boss may say to a subordinate, "Shape up or ship out." This statement rests on the assumption that the command itself is strong enough to produce the desired behavior even though to do so may put the subordinate at odds with his whole group.

The strategy of changing behavior by "decree" is seen in the "a new boss sweeps clean" approach. A new boss takes over a job, sees things not to his or her liking, imposes his or her will on the situation, and tells people in a direct way to stop doing what they have been doing and to start doing what the boss wants done. The boss is using power and authority to break up prevailing norms. This method is sometimes successful, but far more often it fails. Those whose behavior it is expected to shift often resist. Though subordinates may not recognize that fact, they prefer to act in accordance with the prevailing norms that are held in place by the influence of colleagues rather than to follow a boss's directives. More often than not, they simply use passive resistance, although sometimes their resistance goes underground. Eventually the new boss comes to terms with it by recognizing his or her inability to introduce change rapidly. Resistance to change has set in. Productivity remains at about the same level as before.

The following case study accurately depicts this notion in a situation in which a cultural norm had been established for wage workers to leave the job early and no one supervisor wished to draw the line and take the risk of being seen as a "dictator" by the troops. It became a matter of having all the supervisors become committed to superordinate goals of corporate excellence to resolve the early quitting problem.

Case Study: Getting More Productivity from the Last Hour of Work[1]

One of the most difficult changes to implement is one that replaces a past practice with a new policy requiring people to put forth more effort. Such was the situation in this case where upper level management recognized a problem and decided to correct it. They realized that both supervisors and employees would probably be opposed to it. Therefore they tried to communicate to the supervisors and sell them on the need to change. The supervisors did not resist, but the problem remained.

Employees in one plant of the Paterno Company had fallen into the habit of slacking off during the last hour of work. Supervisors were aware of this and were under a good deal of pressure from their managers to do something about it. Privately they acknowledged it as a real problem, but in fact they did nothing. Rather, they scheduled themselves into their offices during the last hour of the day under the guise of using that hour for planning the next day's work. The result was that they didn't have to see the problem. At first, the supervisors felt it was a temporary situation and would correct itself. However, it continued for three years and became a chronic issue.

An unusual situation existed that complicated the problem. Employees had work-related justifications for being away from their primary area and in contact with employees in different sections. Thus employees in any supervisory area might be supervised by that area's supervisor or by a supervisor from another area.

The Situation

In diagnosing the situation, management realized that the problem was out of control. Original policy had been replaced by a norm that legitimized slacking off as a way of slowing down. The problem reflected poor management. It also had an adverse effect on morale and productivity because employees lined up in front of the time clock instead of staying at their workplace until it was time to punch out.

Rather than exercise responsibility for achieving productivity, none of the supervisors took corrective action to rectify the problem. Each one intuitively sensed that to take such an action would be unpopular and would probably bring criticism from both supervisory colleagues and from employees for trying to win points with management; this is the conformity pressure problem.

They understood that if the boss never saw them in the area where social activities were taking place, no manager could complain that the supervisor "was right there and saw the problem and did nothing about it." This was particularly true if supervisors could justify their absence from the field of activity because they were "planning tomorrow's work."

The problem of slacking off was seen to represent a breakdown in supervisory effectiveness. Needed was the establishment of a new norm, accepted fully by all supervisors, so that each could feel support from the others in acting more responsibly in solving the problem. With such a norm in place, any supervisor who failed to exercise responsibility for correcting the problem would become the deviant. The problem, therefore, was to help supervisors replace the "do nothing" norm with a norm of shared responsibility for maintaining productivity throughout the workday.

Twenty of these supervisors reported to four managers. Over the last several years, the managers repeatedly discussed the problem among themselves. Different approaches to its resolution were attempted one after another, all without measurable success. One approach called for each manager to talk to his or her supervisors and explain the importance of having people apply their efforts during the last work hour. Each manager did this and requested each supervisor's help in resolving the difficulty. Nothing happened.

A second approach discussed by the managers was whether a symbolic firing of one or two supervisors might not signal to the rest that "we mean business." If this "message" could get through to supervisors, it might settle the problem once and for all. This solution was not applied, however, because of fear that such firings would be demoralizing and would lead to even further reductions in productivity. Another possible approach was to employ two new supervisors who were not privy to past practices and who would therefore be freer to take the lead in bringing about needed changes.

Other possible solutions were discussed or tried, but none provided a satisfactory resolution of the problem. Finally, management made a determined effort to turn things around. They instituted a series of meetings. The participants in this case were the twenty supervisors. They were in a position to resolve the problem, and it was their responsibility to do so. Moreover, all of them needed to be involved in formulating and maintaining the new norm. All had completed Grids and knew the new way of thinking. Even then, however, it was necessary to rely on consultant help in implementing this first major application. Others that followed were designed by internal consultants.

Identifying the Problem

The first action with the supervisors was to identify the causes of the problem in response to the following questions, written on flip-chart paper: "What are the causes for the slacking-off problem? How can they be rectified?" Supervisors convened during the last hour of work to deal with these questions. Since the "do nothing" norm was shared by all the supervisors, they were gathered together in two leaderless groups of ten to discuss the problem.

It wasn't difficult for the discussion to get going. One supervisor said, "Attitudes toward work have changed. It's not like the old days. People expect to find more enjoyment nowadays and that's why they slow down." Another said, "The workers are older now. They feel their jobs are secure. They don't have to prove that they are hard workers. They know that they have jobs that will carry them to retirement if they wish to stay aboard." A third said, "The work they do isn't terribly interesting. Concentrating on it seven hours a day is a pretty good achievement. Slowing down during the last hour is very understandable." A fourth said, "The real problem is the new generation. It has a more casual attitude than the last generation and it has infected everyone. It's a hopeless situation."

The "them-ism" problem was apparent. Each supervisor was putting the blame on "them." Each of the "them-ism" explanations was recorded on a flip chart for all to see. Finally, a different explanation was offered tentatively by one of the supervisors, who said, "When you come right down to it, the problem is that we're not supervising." Another quickly said, "Don't write that down. We don't want anybody to see that!" However, once the real issue had been exposed, it was not so easily dismissed. Supervisors finally faced up to their responsibility, and the consultant was authorized to commit this fundamental admission to paper. As the discussion continued, participants centered on the "we're not supervising" explanation of the problem. Someone else then asked, "If we are not supervising, why aren't we supervising? We are paid to be supervisors." The discussion had now identified the "do nothing" norm. Each participant could verify it in terms of his or her own reality.

The discussion became more involved as the supervisors zeroed in on their own feelings. Someone said, "I know that none of you will do anything about the problem, and therefore if I do, all I'll get in return is kidding by the rest of you and criticism by employees. Why should I expose myself to that kind of hassle when I don't have to?" Others readily agreed. The general feeling emerged that none of the supervisors was confident of the readiness of other supervisors to come to grips with the problem. The cause had finally been identified.

Action Planning for Resolution

The next meeting dealt with exploring solutions to the problem. After some discussion, one supervisor made the following point: "I'm willing to take the initiative in solving the problem in my area, but only if the rest of you are willing to do likewise in your areas. I'm not going to do it if you're not going to." This comment introduced a very intense discussion of the extent to which supervisors would be willing to commit themselves to a new norm related to maintaining productivity throughout the workday. Some supervisors were reluctant to commit themselves to it for fear of a backlash.

As the meeting continued, the new norm began to emerge, but it was obvious that supervisors were unprepared to give their support to it until they had explored how it might be implemented. As the possibility was discussed, an idea developed that implementation should take place in a stepwise way. Much discussion led to the formulation of the following action plan.

- *Week 1:* Every supervisor meets with his or her employees to announce that supervisors across the organization have agreed that it is their responsibility to provide leadership in solving the slacking-off problem. Supervisors have uniformly committed themselves to doing so. During this week supervisors ask employees to talk with one another and hopefully to give favorable consideration to helping them bring the problem to a constructive solution.

- *Week 2:* Supervisors begin implementing the new norm by becoming active in their work areas. When they see someone being sociable in an unproductive way, they ask the person to return to work but take no further action.

- *Week 3:* Supervisors ask each person they see socializing in an unproductive way to get back to work, and they record the person's name if they know it, or ask the person his or her name if they don't. They report the person's name to the appropriate supervisor.

- *Week 4:* If the problem persists, the supervisors interview those who are socializing in an unproductive way in order to make sure that the slackers understand the seriousness of the intent to solve the problem.

- *Week 5:* If an employee persists in slacking off, a letter is placed in the file as a documentation preparatory to disciplinary action.

- *Week 6:* If the behavior continues, the supervisor takes disciplinary action.

Development of this action plan proved to supervisors that a positive solution was feasible. By this time all supervisors had committed themselves to the new norm and to its implementation.

Implementing the Plan

During the first two weeks, the slacking-off phenomenon became the butt of considerable joking, not only among the hourly personnel but also between the workers and their supervisors. Remarks were made like, "Am I being sociable or is this a legitimate problem for us to be discussing?" However, it was evident that the announcement by the supervisors that they were committed to solving the problem was enough to clear the air and develop a widely shared positive attitude toward improving the situation. A few nudgings were necessary during the third week, but the problem had diminished to such a degree that no interviews were necessary, no letters of documentation were placed in the files, and no disciplinary action was undertaken.

The supervisors reconvened twice to review the situation— once at the end of the third week and once at the end of the seventh week. They experienced great satisfaction that the problem had been solved and, beyond that, saw the importance of leading employees in a responsible way and supporting one another in the process of doing so.

The opposite of a backlash effect was observed because morale seemed to improve among supervisors and employees alike. One employee said, "To tell you the truth, I always felt a little guilty toward the end of the day. I knew it wasn't quite right, but everyone else was doing it, so I joined the gang. In fact, time goes by much faster when I have something to do."

This approach to the slacking-off problem is a good example of how norm shifting can be used to replace the "do nothing" norm that had been held in place by distrust. Any effort to solve the problem without replacing the "do nothing" norm was bound to have been unsuccessful simply because the true cause of the problem had not been diagnosed. Bringing the distrust that supervisors felt toward one another into focus provided the necessary insight and motivation to deal constructively with the real issue.

Conclusions

Relying on power and authority to change norms can be risky and often unsuccessful. Over and above the resistance it provokes, whether active or passive, there is the likelihood of alienating those who are expected to shift their behavior. These people may become resentful and even vengeful. Significantly lowered morale may make it even more difficult to realize the sought-after improvements.

Many bosses in a new assignment realize that their power and authority are weak, or perhaps they sense the adverse consequences that can arise from resistance to change. What do they do under these circumstances? Perhaps we might gain some understanding of the forces that operate by looking at another setting.

Managers in a new assignment may seek to exert influence but do little more to make their influence felt than change job titles or add a little bit of office decoration. The takeover is symbolic. Such a boss may wait several months until he or she has learned the ropes before trying to introduce real changes. The "go slow" boss learns the norms and standards that prevailed before attempting to introduce changes. However, the boss is more than likely to adopt the prevailing norms and standards. The result is that this manager becomes the spokesperson for the normative culture of the group and ultimately becomes part of that culture without exerting further influence thereafter.

An alternative to exercising power and authority to command change is to use the knowledge we now have of norms and their influence on behavior to moderate behavior change. The way to change norms is to involve those whose behavior is regulated by them in studying what the existing norms are and exploring alternatives that might better serve corporate objectives. This is what happened in the case of the supervisors described earlier. Only after prevailing norms are understood can specific steps necessary for shifting from the old to the new be considered and implemented. In changing a norm, the key is to involve those who are controlled by the norm itself. When the norm is shifted, altered attitudes and behavior consistent with the new attitudes can be expected to emerge.

The following conditions are basic to success.

1. *All norms carriers actively participate:* Both primary and reference group members who are carriers of the prevailing norm must actively participate. It is their support of new patterns of behavior or new norms of productivity (volume, quality, control of waste, and so on) that governs whether new approaches will prevail.

2. *Leadership is by those responsible for ultimate decisions:* There is no realistic prospect for changing norms and standards if the leaders of the prevailing norm system absent themselves from the effort. Obviously, if they do not think through the prevailing norms and the behavior limitations that the norms create, they are in no position to give their leadership approval to identifying and developing new and more appropriate norms.

3. *Participants are involved with the problem:* Norms are likely to be anything but explicit and self-evident. There-

fore the problem is how to identify them so that they can be dealt with objectively.

4. *Facts and data are provided about the objective situation:* If norms have been based on false information, providing participants with objective evidence of the true state of affairs can facilitate the rejection of the old norm and the acceptance of one that squares better with the facts.

5. *Ventilation and catharsis are provided as needed:* Those involved in a problem—both employees who practice the unproductive behavior and those who are responsible for it—are often frustrated by its continued existence. They blame others for it. Without the opportunity to get their frustrations and antagonisms into the open, they continue to find it difficult to think constructively about how the problem might be resolved. Thus an atmosphere that allows those who are a part of the problem to discharge their feelings and emotions is essential. Only in this way can they get rid of the negative attitudes that are preventing constructive problem solving. Such emotions and feelings constitute evidence that members share a norm, one that they are likely to impose on one another in a way that makes a deviant suspect.

6. *Reasons for the current problems are identified:* Participants often have different explanations of a problem. Discussion separates false from valid explanations.

7. *Implicit agreements are made explicit:* Whatever the discussions produce by way of proposed new attitudes and behaviors, the conclusions that are reached need to be crystallized and validated by public agreement rather than simply presumed to be widely acceptable.

8. *Changes in norms are subject to follow-up:* In the beginning, new norms are weaker than those they replace. The result is that people tend to backslide toward the norm that previously prevailed. Follow-up to strengthen new attitudes and behavior and bring them into effective use is essential.

Summary

The kind of problems discussed in this chapter, such as the

one portrayed in the preceding case study, illustrate the working material for Phase 1A projects. They are superordinate problems, arising out of the organization culture, belonging to no one in particular, yet adverse to sound business practices. Once managers have had the opportunity to experience working effectively in a group to achieve concrete objectives, they are motivated to put these new skills into practice. They are primed for Phase 2, Team Building; however, they may need to defer this process until colleagues in their teams have completed the same foundation learning experience. It is at this point that Phase 1A projects can be brought in to signal the beginning of concrete change, adding further fuel to the already kindled fires of motivation and commitment.

In Chapter 7, we take a look at Phase 2—the Team Building activity—where this same enthusiasm is taken into the team and the focus shifted to issues that serve to enhance the functioning and effectiveness of the team itself.

Reference

1. The case study presented in this chapter is taken from our work in Kirkpatrick, D. L. 1985. *How to Manage Change Effectively.* San Francisco: Jossey-Bass.

7

Team Building

The culture of a company and, more particularly, its human values can be seen in purest form in the team formations within which executives, managers, supervisors, and employees work on a continuous basis. These are "family" or nuclear groups whose members are permanent and clustered around a common center of organization responsibility. For example, a corporate CEO and his or her direct reports constitute the top team of a company. An intricate web of attitudes, beliefs, and values can be seen in their problem-solving interrelationships. Traditions, rules of thumb, and assumptions are used in making decisions and resolving differences. All are attributes of team culture.

One characteristic of corporate teams that distinguishes them from groups is the degree to which productivity values and purposes are shared. If team members have difficulty in agreeing on purpose or are found to have widely differing values, they are likely to have more difficulty in coming to agreement. That is not to say that teams should brainwash themselves to one model of organization thinking. Differences are healthy and stimulating in open, candid, and conflict-solving relationships.

However, there is room to bring out the silent or unstated assumptions that may be interfering with team progress and intellectually replace them with ones that might lead to greater understanding. Even airing of those assumptions *without changing them* can contribute to trust and mutual respect. The unknown stimuli of differences become known and, consequently, behavior becomes less sinister and more understandable. Expectations are no longer violated. Courses of action can be chosen that have a superordinate quality—the best of several worlds.

The following example shows how team culture can affect a work team. It takes place at Apple Computer, shortly after John Sculley has been recruited by Steve Jobs to get a handle on the management side of this rapidly growing firm. This is the teamwork that characterized Apple upon Sculley's arrival.

> I tried to direct the discussion around these and other issues placed on the agenda, but it was to no avail. The meeting became a free-for-all. Whoever could attract the group's attention controlled the floor. It was difficult to distinguish between facts and opinions. People would have side conversations during executive presentations; some would get up from their places to get something. It was virtually impossible to keep order.
>
> It became a finger-pointing, no-holds-barred session. It became clear that this wasn't a team at all; that we had a group of individuals, all running their own functions. People felt free to say anything they wanted to say about anyone or anything, and they often vented issues and attacked each other.
>
> Many of them traded insults as often as kids do when trading baseball cards.
>
> "You were wrong about this last time," one executive would shout to another.
>
> "Well, I think you're the most incompetent manager that's ever come to Apple," he would retort.
>
> "What makes you the expert on competence?"[1]

If Sculley had questioned any of the members of this team about the quality of their teamwork process, they would have insisted that it was characterized by openness and candor. This hardly appears to be the case, however, illustrating once again the pervasive nature of self-deception.

Phase 2, Team Building, involves refinement and strengthening of teamwork processes. It helps teams identify constraints to excellence present in their own conduct of the business. Furthermore, it can help them to project actions that can provide a basis for each individual to make a maximum corporate contribution. It is a way of X-raying actions of every team member in order to pinpoint strengths and weaknesses.

Another benefit in Team Building is the development of conflict resolution skills. Objectives are made clear and the "rules of the game" are known in advance. Then they can be revised if they constitute impediments. Creativity and productivity are enhanced since conflict is no longer shunned; openness and candor serve as a source of stimulation and emergent ideas—something that is relished by the team as an opportunity for innovation.

Team Building can be compared to the video used in the recurrent cockpit training described earlier. Likewise, it resembles a football game replay which permits for analysis, study, and correction of the calls. Through careful study, performance can be examined for the quality of teamwork present, and members can assess how well efforts are coordinated, how flexibly unforeseen opportunities are seized upon, and whether or not team effort is dynamic or mechanical in nature. By critiquing strengths and weaknesses and by seeing options that might be acted upon, team members learn much about the productivity and quality of their performance. Inadequacies can be identified and eliminated; strengths can be consolidated and reinforced.

Team Building offers a way of grappling with cultural barriers to team effort which must be resolved in the pursuit of corporate excellence. It is a first major step of organization application of the Grid concepts learned in Phase 1 and the preliminary work of Phase 1A projects.

The Team Building activities are divided into several segments that emphasize a number of key team dimensions, which are discussed in more detail in the case study that follows. Briefly, however, they are

1. the power and authority exercised by the boss,
2. the norms and standards a team has adopted that influence members' attitudes and behavior,
3. the goals and objectives that address the purpose of the team,
4. the cohesion and morale that serve to unite or divide members,
5. differentiation and structure of the activities of team members, and

6. feedback and critique to individual members and the team as a whole that provide for improvement in team effectiveness.

The last dimension, feedback and critique, is key. Feedback and critique are used throughout each activity to aid in steering team development and to enable members to develop process skills for effective problem solving. Team Building activities follow a deliberate sequence, which starts with an audit of the present and extends to development of relevant issues centered in the future. Since teams may differ in terms of the depth and breadth of issues, topics discussed and time spent on each dimension may vary.

Strengthening Team Culture

Teamwork development is not left to chance; neither is it left to happen, such as in in situ development. To accomplish the desired ends, it is an organized and well-planned activity. Just as in the Grid Seminar training, Team Building begins with prework. Each team member reads *Spectacular Teamwork*[2] and then completes a series of instruments that provide perspective on the quality and character of team action and individual efforts. This includes how team members see themselves operating as well as what other team members are doing or are not doing that furthers or reduces the effectiveness of the team.

Completing this series of Grid instruments forms a conceptual and operational foundation. The real learning, however, takes place when all members of the team meet to study and resolve team problems. For a period of about three days, inquiry into team effectiveness involves study of each member's view of the team culture based on the six dimensions already mentioned. It provides each team a model of how to go about solving new problems that emerge in the future.

Implications

Team Building starts at the top. Four to six weeks later, each of the top team subordinates, as head of his or her own team, convenes with subordinates to study their teams' effectiveness. Most organization members complete two Team Building activities. One is in the team where he or she is a subordinate and the second involves the team where he or she is boss. Team Building is not a one-shot affair but may be repeated whenever it seems appropriate to ensure that high-quality results are constantly being maintained. Apart from the effectiveness issue, induction teamwork development may be scheduled after a significant shift in original team membership has occurred.

Participation Is Not Enough

Through such effort, team members characteristically come to have a far deeper sense of self-esteem and commitment to organization success above and beyond their own narrow self-interests. The Team Building activities place a premium on participation. The purposes cannot be realized without open, candid, and committed participation. Participation, however, is not a solution in and of itself.

Participation is often touted as an important answer to corporate problems. Without a doubt, it can be a powerful antidote to win/lose competitiveness and complacency. It awakens feelings of ownership, evoking involvement and commitment to achieving the corporate objectives so essential to success. It leads to creativity and innovation, and to expanding the flexibility with which managers approach the exercise of leadership.

Why then is participation not the cure, particularly if it can accomplish such seemingly useful objectives? We often hear that much of the frustration associated with organization life can be alleviated if only people have opportunities to participate in making decisions that affect them. But this does not always prove to be the case. The Grid is useful in getting at the heart of this question. "Participation" can take place under any Grid style, except perhaps the 1,1 position. The particular form it takes, however, affects the consequences of its use. Some forms of participation result in very unhealthy consequences.

For these reasons, participation is no panacea. Under some circumstances it can prove to be valuable, but deeper analysis suggests that it is *not* participation in and of itself that leads to the values behind involvement, commitment, and dedication. Rather, what produces these human motivations is challenging goals and objectives, the opportunity to contribute one's thoughts and energies toward their accomplishment, and a situation that recognizes and rewards meritorious performance. Active, strong participation in problem solving is central to this, but it is these several factors in conjunction with one another that awaken feelings of membership, responsibility, and the strong desire to contribute.

The following case study is a continuation of the story introduced in Chapter 4 involving Quinn Morton's top team, where I got started as a long-term consultant to the company through an extended stint as a participant-observer.

Case Study:

Acting as a participant-observer, I had made a practice of joining the top team for meetings, whether impromptu or planned, operating as a silent observer and taking no active part in projects currently underway or on the drawing board. This provided an excellent window for checking out my understanding of what I had heard about the top team's performance from some of its individual members.

Needless to say, many of the observations reported were confirmed but, equally so, numerous other significant features of that top team's performance had not yet been brought to my attention. That is the merit of participant observation. One can observe directly rather than relying on second-hand reports.

Team Diagnosis

At the end of two months, I broke my silence and convened a session of the top team where I spent a considerable period of time reviewing what I had learned. Some of the main features are summarized here. Before doing so, however, I need to provide one additional degree of background, a framework to order these observations in a more systematic manner. This framework provides the basis for the Phase 2 Team Building activity.

Over the years, we have come to rely on six key dimensions of team action as the framework for structuring our observations. These dimensions are basic and comprehensive.

1. It is apparent that every team relies on some variant of power and authority to provide leadership. In this team, consider Quinn's character of leadership. He was seen by

all members, and himself as well, as a truly dedicated professional manager whose purpose was to meld his organization and his executive team into the most effective unit possible in order to lead the company. He was a chemical engineer by training and, based on his natural brilliance, qualified in every sense to do so.

His main limitation lay in the area of power and authority. His overattention to detail impacted the team in an adverse way. The following illustrates this point.

Quinn conducted meetings more or less on a go-around-the-table basis, asking each subordinate for a detailed accounting of what was happening in his or her department or division. Sometimes the level of discussion got down to trivia, and an excessive amount of time was spent in one-on-one discussion while others simply observed. Discussions generally took on a win/lose flavor. During these interrogations, Quinn seemed to get a kick out of tracking facts down to their roots and then adding a new piece of evidence picked up from his own background. This gave him the sense of winning, though I must say he was never hostile or vindictive about it.

2. The second major dimension of teamwork relates to norms and standards, those uniformities of attitude and behavior that team members have come to accept as characteristic ways of thinking and behaving in that team. The equivalent word is "culture" so far as uniformities are concerned, but of course culture includes all dimensions being discussed rather than being restricted to norms and standards.

A dominant norm or standard in this team is the norm of thoroughness. In personal discussions, Quinn repeatedly mentioned how important he saw it to be for members of the team to be thorough and comprehensive in their knowledge of that piece of the action for which they were responsible. This ties in with Quinn's interrogatory approach in that his way of teaching thoroughness was to keep people on their toes.

A side effect of this norm as it affected teamwork was that each subordinate replicated in his or her own leadership much the same behavior they experienced from Quinn. They would each assemble their teams and have highly technical reviews in order to marshal the information they felt necessary in order to placate Quinn. When asked about the norm of thoroughness, one said, "Quinn may be operating by a thoroughness norm, but we rely on the defensiveness norm. We keep on digging, not necessarily because we think this focus on detail contributes to corporate ends but because we need it to contend with Quinn in those meetings." Quinn's compulsions about the technical side of engineering, in other words, were having unanticipated side effects that were not in the best interest of the firm.

3. Vision, purpose, the future—all of these are terms that aid in speaking about what any organization is attempting to accomplish. They are its goals and objectives. I think Quinn's goals and objectives were clear as he expressed them to me when I took on the project. He said, in effect, "I want to see how good we can make this company if we go all out." He often repeated the same goal to his executive team.

The difficulty in interpreting this statement is that it seemed at variance with actual behavior. What others perceived as his two primary goals were the exercise of technical prowess and having everyone on the team think exactly as he did. This left much to be desired in terms of effective use of human resources. Furthermore, while Quinn was something of a genius when it came to planning and designing broad strategies, he did this more or less as an unshared activity. His plans were announced by edict, providing little opportunity for people to challenge his intended direction. The very nature of Quinn's leadership created a reactive rather than proactive top team. Such a team becomes reluctant to take risks.

4. Cohesion and morale relate to the attractiveness of the team to its individual members. In my view, the level of cohesion and morale in this group was moderately high. In part this was based on the company's success, Quinn's respected intellectual strength, the competence of other members, and the high-tech quality of the company.

5. Differentiation and structure refer to how team activities are divided up and spread out among members. There seemed to be no major problems here, but there is a problem in the way in which structure is being used for control as revealed in the actual discussion reported later.

6. The use of feedback and critique by members to help one another be more effective and to introduce corrections into operational activities was practically unknown to the top team. Performance reviews were held on a one-to-one basis, but there was no norm or standard that said, in effect, "Our goal is to share experiences and learn from one another." My observations told me that this was a serious limitation in the effectiveness of this top team.

Based on the discussion I had requested with the team, the decision was quickly reached to engage in a Team Building experience for several consecutive days including night meetings. An outside setting was chosen and a time agreed upon. The major obstacle that had to be overcome to bring this Team Building activity to fruition was how to keep the firm on steady course with the top 13 people absent. This led to a discussion of whether or not it was too risky to make the attempt, no matter how desirable it otherwise might be, and how to deal with emergencies from a remote location without excessively interrupting the Team Building activity, while at the same time retaining responsibility for major organizational problem solving.

Team Building began with individual members completing prework items, characterizing how each one saw the team in terms of the six dimensions. Each person completed the instruments and provided verbal vignettes to indicate why the scale was completed in the manner reported. The Team Building activities themselves were based on an open discussion of each person's views according to these six dimensions, with planning for how they should be operating as a team were they able to overcome the existing impediments to full effectiveness.

Team Building often has an uneasy beginning simply because people may never have participated in such an activity before. They may feel anxious and uncertain, not knowing quite what to expect. Most team cultures do not immediately embrace the concepts of rigorous honesty.

I took the initiative in providing an orientation by clarifying what had previously been discussed, i.e., the six dimensions to set the stage for organizing the discussion with concrete evidence to be provided in order to avoid empty generalities. I said that the discussion of the six dimensions had no particular sequence and we could start wherever it seemed most sensible. I added that the discussion was intended to be freewheeling.

Quinn then took over and said he did not intend to exercise leadership as was done in routine business meetings. This brought forth a good deal of laughter but also some pointed comments, such as, "We hear your words, Quinn, but we know you by your deeds."

The discussion then got underway. A member said, "I have what I think is a fundamental observation. I think it's concerned with *differentiation* and *structure*, but that's not particularly relevant." Attention was focused on this individual, who was respected by the whole group. He continued, "I think our key problem was clearly evident when we began discussing Team Building several weeks ago. I've given this a considerable amount of thought.

"We were scared to death of the idea of leaving the firm for three or four days en masse for fear that something might happen in our absence. We believed that those who remained might not be able to handle the day-to-day problems. This, it seems to me, is a real weakness in our organization. I see it as a failure on our part to have effectively sorted out what we should be doing from what we shouldn't be doing. As a result of this, we have also failed to develop subordinates in ways that could provide corporate strength at the operational and executional levels. In other words, as a top team, we have performed poorly in the sense that we have done insufficient strategy planning. We have been too busy with nuts and bolts."

This basic point was to reappear again and again, and it became the main issue in some fundamental revisions of how the top team is now performing. Identification of this problem led directly into Quinn's exercise of power and authority. The team concluded by saying, "Quinn, as long as you persist in interrogating us on the technical side, we will never solve this problem of delegation. We find it necessary to be informed of every detail in order to 'perform' for you. If we spend all our time 'prepping' in order to second-guess your questions, there is little time left for strategic planning. You are left alone to do that; it's not something we do as a team to maximally synergize our future thinking. Until you decide to involve us in strategic planning, we are nothing but technicians."

All of this was reinforced through deliberating, "What's the norms and standards issue?"

"You say that you're out to promote thoroughness. We say, in effect, you are producing defensiveness. The defensiveness results in thoroughness but on the wrong projects and for the wrong reasons."

The feedback to one another and the critique of how the team's performance might be characterized and shifted was of good quality. There was no question but that the team was grappling with the fundamental problems of its effectiveness in an open and candid way that promised hope for the future. Resolution of the delegation problem seemed to be prerequuisite to getting into strategic planning.

Finally, on the third day, after much further discussion of these and other dimensions, a conclusion was formulated. "We'd like to give ourselves three months to solve the delegation problem with our own people. That brings us to the month of April. At this time, Quinn, you will have kept your commitment to the revised agenda to which we have agreed. We commit ourselves to a broad basis of discussion of next steps down through the rest of the firm and to getting started on strategic planning in April." This was seen as a very satisfying conclusion to all involved. A plan of action had been laid out.

This Phase 2 episode portrays some of the problems facing the top management team in one organization. Different problems confront different teams but the process of working them through follows along these lines.

Communication is a problem in many instances. The solution to it lies in invoking different theories of managerial behavior than those that managers have unwittingly applied in the past. The use of the 9,9 theory increases the prospect that mutual human understanding will be achieved. With mutual understanding, the likelihood is increased that unobstructed communication can take place and stronger and more worthy objectives can be set. With shared commitment to attaining these objectives, we can realistically expect improved results.

Difficulties of planning are also reflected in the case study. The solution depends on solving the communication problem. Once the communication problem has been dealt with, a foundation of interaction has been laid for sound planning and for achieving commitment to the execution of plans that can have operational consequences in terms of bottom-line results.

Without planned, deliberate, organized follow-up, the insights into managerial behavior acquired from a Grid Seminar are unlikely to find their way into operational action. Team Building can increase the likelihood that behavior theories will be instituted into daily use by contributing to the removal of operational barriers to excellence.

Team Building With Non-Intact Teams

A further word is appropriate in the context of the cockpit development project. Following the initial seminars in which all pilots engaged, another well-known OD principle came clearly into focus. That is, a training intervention in and of itself is rarely long enough or basic enough to bring about an immediate and effective turnaround in anything so deep as a cockpit culture, particularly with shifting membership in teams. Thus Team Building to deepen Grid understandings as they affect cockpit safety practices was seen as the logical extension, or the second stage of organization development.

This step in the process is undertaken in the simulators used for training pilots in 727s, 747s, and so on. During the flight, the instrument presentations and circumstances that the crews encounter create "difficulties" that test their effectiveness under non-routine circumstances. Crew members are aware that a video camera has been mounted in the back of the cockpit, and they can view the videotape later as first-hand evidence of their effectiveness in dealing with the situation. The simulator instructor records the critical incidents to be focused on in critique. These points are made known when crew members receive the videotape for personal review.

Crews then assemble, usually as three-person groups, each responsible for conducting its own critique. The tape is played, with particular attention placed on critical incidents that reveal issues of teamwork effectiveness. Crews play the tape, discuss it, rewind it, and play it again—sometimes repeatedly until a consensus is reached among the group as to what happened. They also seek to determine the soundest handling of the circumstance as it took place. A standard reaction observed in crew after crew is that seeing themselves and their interactions under simulator conditions approximates the "real thing." Therefore it offers validating evidence as to the importance of effective teamwork, along with skill in implementing it.

In this way, crews were given the opportunity to apply what they had learned from their initial training intervention to an "on-the-job" setting by solving dilemmas in actual flight simulators. The testing and reinforcement of leadership principles under near-flight conditions were sufficient to strengthen the shared readiness to implement a two o'clock (open cockpit) culture. Yearly reinforcement of these principles under flight simulator conditions is still underway and expected to continue.

The Grid training is required for all United Airlines pilots and is currently in use by over 5000 flying personnel from domestic and international carriers as well as many from corporate aviation and the military. Most of these follow up with recurrent training of the kind described here where crews work through incidents or scenarios in a flight simulator and then critique how well they use the available resources.

The idea of resource management has spread to other fields as well. The following excerpt from the Medical Grid program[3] demonstrates this same concern for sound teamwork in the medical setting.

> As the leader of the team, you have to understand the human needs of those people you are working with as well as the medical-technical expertise they contribute to the care you provide. Acquiring personal information from those individuals who work with you is often overlooked, as physicians

tend to concentrate on technical matters. Decisions that create the working conditions of your program impact every member of your medical team, yet unilateral decision making may have become an ingrained habit. In this case, the opinion of your experienced medical staff is lost. Conflict resolution is critical in shaping your working environment. If your response to conflict is to initiate critique and feedback, your team is actually able to grow and create new solutions to the unanticipated problems that constantly face you.

Carrying working conditions one step further, you have to look specifically at the hospitals where you deliver medical care. The priority that the hospital has given your particular subspecialty will dictate what equipment and facilities are available to help meet the medical-technical needs of your patients. Equally important is a commitment to staff development, which may or may not make meeting the human need a particular challenge. But, through all of this, it is important to remember that no physician is a victim of circumstance. Through effective leadership skills, you can organize your peers and create working conditions that support a 9,9 medical practice.

The reality of modern medical care is that it cannot be accomplished alone. The era of one physician with a horse and buggy moving from home to home on the open frontier is long behind us. Today the complex interactions of physician, physician extender, nurse, hospital administrator, third-party payor, patient, and family support structure for the patient are inextricable.

When you ask, "What type of people do I want to work with as I attempt to establish my 9,9 medical practice?," try to keep your thinking simple. Ask what kind of people you like to work with. Find people who are optimistic, who have smiles on their faces, who believe that quality medical care is possible. A good way to determine what type of individuals you need for a supportive medical team is to ask the opposite question. "What type of individuals would totally devastate my program?" Another is, "What characteristics of people would prevent 9,9 teamwork?" Common replies are often dishonesty, narrowness, unreliability, and so on. Simply looking for the opposite qualities, we find honest individuals who are broad thinkers and reliable when it comes to task performance.

Apart from general management, three new areas of recent application beyond the cockpit in which we are involved include the air traffic controller group, the aerospace industry, and the nuclear control room floor. The teams in this latter group tend to be more intact as working groups than those previously mentioned. Yet, the problem is the same: "How do we maximize the resources of team members in order to achieve the soundest and safest outcome?"

Regardless of the task activity with which team members must deal, difficulties in effectively meshing resources appear and reappear. This important generalization leads to the conclusion that teamwork development provides a significant opportunity for increased effectiveness regardless of the work context within which it appears.

Summary

We have sought to convey the significance of Phase 2, Team Building, of Grid Organization Development. When organization members come face to face with solving problems that limit effectiveness, they often find that the demands on them for the initiative, energy, and genuine commitment to organization objectives are substantial. The motivation for making the effort is "theirs." The shift, or tip-over, from old to new, from competitive back biting or indifference to a spirit of collaborative effort, is well underway.

References

1. Sculley, J., with J. A. Byrne. 1987. *Odyssey: Pepsi to Apple ... A Journey of Adventure, Ideas, and the Future.* New York: Harper & Row, p. 128.

2. Blake, R. R., J. S. Mouton, and R. L. Allen. 1987. *Spectacular Teamwork.* New York: John Wiley & Sons.

3. Prather, S. E., R. R. Blake, and J. S. Mouton. 1988. *Caring for Difficult Patients: Beyond Medical Excellence Through Physician Leadership.* Austin: Scientific Methods, Inc., pp. 124, 125. (unpublished work)

8

Interface Conflict-Solving Model

Not all problems in the behavior dynamics of a firm are to be found in natural work teams. Another dimension exists that cuts through the organization both laterally and vertically: breakdowns of cooperation and trust at organizational interfaces. An *interface* is any point of contact between organized groups at which interchanges are necessary to achieve a desired result. The points of contact are between departments, divisions, and regions. They involve the dynamics between groups rather than interpersonal relationships (as in Team Building). Issues of organizational effectiveness present in the interface contacts include information flow, coordination arrangements, and decision making.

Everyday examples are commonplace. They can be found between marketing and product development, between sales and manufacturing, between MIS and inventory control, between programmers and end users. Tensions often exist between the human resources group and various operating departments. Others, more subdued in the past decade but promising a renewal of strength in the future, are those between union and management and between operating units and federal agencies of various sorts, particularly those that regulate safe industrial practices. Interfaces of this sort are also observed between manufacturing and the supplier and between the distribution organization, dealer organizations, franchisees, and so on. Where a particular interface difficulty appears is almost unpredictable; that they may be present in an organization of any size can be accepted as a given.

Breakdowns at organizational interfaces can be seen in

chronic polarizations that erupt in mutual destructiveness. They result in poor decision making, lowered productivity, or internecine warfare and ultimately in reduced profitability. The cooperation needed for success is sacrificed because emphasis is placed on protecting group pride, prerogatives, and priorities.

Practical knowledge of how to restore trust as the basis for achieving improved cooperation at the interfaces has been one of the great missing links in the chain necessary for increasing productivity and quality. The theory and techniques of interface conflict solving now available provide an important management tool for creating and maintaining intergroup cooperation.[1]

Trust in another group's good intentions is vital for cooperation. Intergroup relations are particularly vulnerable to breakdowns in trust and confidence. Once distrust appears, it feeds on itself as a self-fulfilling prophecy. As group members on each side of a cleavage discuss the situation with one another, they further reinforce convictions about the correctness of their suspicions of the other group. Since such distrust is so widespread, it follows that restoring confidence between groups is of primary relevance in contributing to organizational strength and increased profitability.

Achieving effective cooperation when problem-solving relationships have broken down can be extraordinarily complicated. Managers receive essentially no college or business school instruction or in-house training in how to conduct these relationships to keep them healthy; nor do they learn how to rebuild them once they have eroded. As a result, disruptive relationships are widely present, sometimes severely so, such as when a new product launch is sabotaged, when a strike is called, when a subsidiary is sold as a way of getting rid of problems, or when a mass firing of almost 12,000 takes place in a desperate attempt to put new people in charge who "can be expected to cooperate."

The Interface Conflict-Solving Model aids members on both sides of a cleavage to explore the conditions necessary for restoring a sound relationship based on trust and respect. It permits them to deal with the factors that have led to the prevailing distrust and to identify the specific actions for reducing destructiveness and shifting the relationship from what it is to what it can become based on collaboration and problem solving. Designing an implementation strategy and action program to achieve these results is included as a final step.

Diagnosis of the relationship at the interface between any two groups that need to cooperate and coordinate may be a desirable first step in determining whether an interface or some alternative activity might be a useful approach. Data can be gathered through instruments or interviews conducted by line managers, human resources personnel, or outsiders. Each team or its leaders can use these findings as a basis for deciding whether or not to undertake an Interface Conflict-Solving activity. Further diagnostic steps within the model can help those who have the problem discover its causes and plan its solution.

The Interface Conflict-Solving Model derives its strength from the diagnosis it permits participants themselves to make, the discrepancies it brings into focus between what currently exists and what is possible, and the group level of support for change it creates. The design administrator is important but incidental to the result; the design *itself* is the major factor in bringing about change.

Intergroup Dynamics

The dynamics of intergroup cooperation and conflict provide a basis of understanding this area of development in systematic terms. Whenever people are segregated, for example, in a manufacturing organization, they become members of that segment, or come to think and act with a "manufacturing" attitude. The same is true for a marketing, an R&D unit, or for a purchasing department. The greater the morale and esprit de corps within that segment, the more its members identify with it and have a common bond. The values, attitudes, and interpretations of problems that come to be common among its members serve as an important background factor in contacts with people in different departments. The same membership factors are at work in these other components. In addition to sharing a common corporate culture, each segment has its own subculture. The problem was illustrated in the in situ diagnostic example presented in Chapter 4, where a definite rift existing between two plants was brought into clear focus by the union issue.

What happens when a misunderstanding arises between two segments within the greater organizational culture? The marketing organization, for example, needs products of errorless quality and in quantities permitting immediate delivery. This permits competitive pricing while achieving high profit margins, thus allowing the marketing department to expand sales. From a manufacturing organization point of view, however, expenses related to error-free production are inordinately high. The manufacturing organization strives for efficiencies realized from planning and scheduling production according to future delivery targets, not immediate ones. Therefore marketing requests may be seen as unreasonable, unjustified, and arbitrary. The attitude of marketing when it is unable to get what it needs is resentment and frustration toward manufacturing's inefficiency and inability to manage its affairs properly. A boundary is created that separates the two departments between whom cooperation and coordination is vital. This is a major conflict-generating point within many organizations. Learning how to achieve maximum cooperation while maintaining the efficiencies possible from segmenting a company into its natural components is an objective of Interface Conflict-Solving.

Conflict between divisions may take a number of different forms. Win/lose conflict is usually apparent to all, with each unit struggling to maintain its own point of view, whether by fair means or foul, almost without regard for the destruction wrought upon the other. The same is often true between union and management, headquarters and subsidiaries, and so on. These 9,1 clashes may be perceived by some as stimulating, improving cohesion and morale of the separate units as each side draws together to do battle, but the resultant loss of overall corporate effectiveness is enormous.

In 5,5 situations of uneasy truce, where bargaining, compromise, negotiation, and accommodation encourage some degree of cooperation and coordination, problems are resolved mechanically by establishing rules of protocol to determine mutual expectations of what the other will or will not do. Unfortunately such rules may maintain peace but at the cost of institutionalizing rigidity. The price paid therefore is in terms of performance that fails, often by a wide margin, to approach standards of excellence.

Other unsatisfactory solutions may also be apparent. Peaceful coexistence (1,9) may be sought when both sides are prepared to accept mutual support in a pleasant and friendly way, trying to avoid problems that would upset harmonious interrelationships. Once again, peace is maintained, but the potential for achievement is sacrificed.

Still another destructive pattern is in evidence when one group adopts the attitude, "We own you," and the other responds like misbehaving teenagers or with a sulking, defeatist attitude—the model of a relationship when one side is paternalistic and the other resentful but dependent. This shows that paternalism can come to characterize whole groups, not just interpersonal relationships.

Finally, 1,1 is apparent when efforts to solve intergroup problems are totally abandoned. The situation becomes polarized, and people creatively find ways to avoid interacting entirely. Such a "solution" produces duplication of effort, with each department doing for itself rather than working interdependently with the other. The resulting waste of human and material resources and the consequent drain on earnings is justified as less burdensome than the hopeless pursuit of cooperation.

All of these rationalizations evidence failure at intergroup cooperation and coordination of varying degrees of severity. They can be contrasted with a 9,9 approach where similar boundaries exist but where the people have learned to confront conflict and to seek sound resolution. By keeping communication open and candid, facing situations of disagreement and controversy, confronting issues rather than letting them fester into win/lose struggles or adopting an attitude of give-and-take negotiation, people on both sides of the boundary can constructively deal with their problems and needs.

The Interface Conflict-Solving Model is the third phase of activity in the Grid OD approach to corporate excellence. Through Interface Conflict-Solving, managers seek to resolve problems preventing needed cooperation across segmented boundaries wherever they exist.

The Interface Conflict-Solving Model: Six Steps

Interface participants are key members of each group embroiled in the conflict. The group members who participate are regarded by themselves, by others who may not participate, and by the members of the other group as responsible for and capable of making the decisions necessary to bring about change. The critical mass includes all those needed to commit the whole membership to actions and whose voices carry weight in implementing or in vetoing action. In addition, the interface development sessions require group members who are sufficiently familiar with the history of the relationship, current norms, and operating practices to re-create and identify them in practice. Participating group members, in other words, represent a microcosm of the whole but beyond that can commit the entire membership.

An apparent contradiction exists in arranging for people to participate in a process of mutual problem solving when existing frictions and antagonisms between groups reduce any readiness of members to cooperate. Certain minimum conditions are necessary to start this process. One is to gain the commitment of the ultimate level of managerial authority necessary for taking action to shift existing relationships. The second condition is that members of both groups are willing to take part in the activities. This commitment involves no promise that positive consequences will occur but rather the acknowledgment that those responsible are ready to give the process a trial.

The session begins with an orientation to review the objectives, activities, and procedures. Although specifics vary depending on particular problems and needs, the same basic six-step process is applicable to diverse interface conflicts in business, industry, and government.

1. *Developing the optimal model:* Each participating group works separately to create a model of optimal interface effectiveness specific to their problems and needs.

2. *Consolidating the optimal relationship:* A consolidated model of a sound relationship is then generated through the groups' joint efforts.

3. *Describing the actual relationship:* Actual conditions that characterize the relationship are described separately by each group, with members analyzing historical factors that shaped and influenced the relationship.

4. *Consolidating the actual relationship:* The groups' individual perspectives are consolidated into a joint picture that accurately and objectively describes the present.

5. *Planning for change:* Changes to be made in specific, operational terms are jointly agreed on and described in detail. These result in plans for follow-up with this group and those not present.

6. *Progress review and replanning:* Follow-up dates are scheduled for groups to reconvene three to six months after the initial session to review progress, critique their current relationship, and plan the next steps.

Neutral outsiders are present to ensure that the Interface Conflict-Solving Model is employed in such a way as to maximize the likelihood of a successful outcome. Their role is thus to administer the process, whereas the group members themselves are responsible for the content—the specific decisions, the recommendations for future actions, or the conclusions formulated. We sometimes serve in this capacity, but this can also be performed internally. Design administrators may be line managers or human resource personnel from within the organization that are at least as high in rank as the most senior managers of the participating groups. In either case, however, administrators are not members of the participant groups and have no vested interest in any particular outcome. Technical knowledge of building relationships and the theories and principles upon which this process rests is critical, as is a dynamic understanding of intergroup behavior.

A typical Phase 3 activity is illustrated in the following case study. Comtradco is a company that was established early in this century to conduct business in natural fibers—primarily cotton and wool, but also jute, flax, and raw silk. Although its origins were in production, a major portion of its business is now in commodities futures trading. Julian Lombard, chief executive officer, has little patience with performance that falls short of expectations or results that fail to meet objectives. Lombard is accustomed to success and measures diligence and dedication primarily in terms of profit. A powerful force in Comtradco, Lombard initiated the interface intervention recounted here in an international textile division called Worldtex. We were invited to undertake this project by Hal Levinson, the new vice president of human resources. Blake recounts the story.

Case Study: Getting Better Integration Between Headquarters and Field

Lombard summoned Joel Myerson, the senior vice president for Worldtex, to discuss the division's most recent results. The balance sheet in front of Lombard reflected the same distressing slow growth pattern he'd been seeing for months. Frustrated and disappointed, Lombard was looking for answers to critical questions of competence, commitment, and return on investment.

"Some time ago," Lombard began, "we gave you the worldwide textiles group to pull together. Your recommendations and expertise in the trading area shaped the division.

You created the current structure, essentially centralizing many of the functions. You said it would work. Three years have passed and even now we're barely breaking even on this part of the business."

"I know our results aren't what they should be," replied Myerson, "but what more can I do? We're working hard, but we don't seem to be getting anywhere. Our people in the field aren't used to headquarters' guidance yet and, although procedures are in place, sometimes they find ways to get around them."

"I understand that," said Lombard, "but how long can we wait? Policies, guidelines, and procedures are there to be followed. I just learned of a case where two of our domestic locations were bidding against each other for the same order. Do we have so little competition outside that we have to manufacture it internally? We ended up paying 15 percent above market. No wonder you're not making any money! What kind of coordination and direction by headquarters does this indicate? Furthermore, when I'm out in the field, many of those managers say the New York desk people are incompetent. Are they? I want to know what's really going on. What are you doing about these problems?"

"Look," sighed Myerson, "I thought things would work out in time, but they haven't. Maybe we should try something else ... change the structure again."

"No! We've tried all that countless times before—you know it won't help. Something dramatic and constructive has to be done now," replied Lombard "I'm not going to let these problems continue. That's a promise. I want you to think through this whole situation and be prepared to give me a recommendation for corrective action by next Monday. I suggest you talk with Levinson. He stays close to what's going on in all parts of the company, and he might be a good sounding board. Maybe he'll be able to suggest an approach we haven't tried before, like making an example or two of what results from deliberate noncompliance. Since we elevated him to vice president of human resources, I think he has exerted a strong and positive influence."

Perspective from Outside

Five days later, Blake and Mouton were invited to participate in an in-depth discussion with Lombard, Myerson, and Levinson of the problem and the potential of the Interface Conflict-Solving Model for dealing with it. This action was initiated by Levinson who had undertaken such an activity in the company with which he was previously affiliated.

Lombard got right to the point. "What can we expect if we decide to do it? Our files are already bulging with studies full of recommendations and prescriptions. The last thing we need is another study that promises a lot and delivers a little."

"This approach is somewhat different," Blake replied. "It doesn't create reams of paper or try to tell management what should be done. The interface process aids in creating a model for change. It provides a methodology to increase the participants' awareness of the need for change."

Mouton added, "It helps participants understand that corporate history is the real enemy. Then it assists in creating a climate that supports a shift away from the unproductive practices of the past and toward the kinds of attitudes and behaviors that increase the likelihood that your goals will be met."

"Will we have to evolve slowly into what we want to become?" Lombard asked. "Some locations need to show improvement right away."

"Culture is much too powerful to be changed easily," Mouton answered. "Lasting results require consistent effort and ongoing follow-up, but you can make a beginning in just a few days."

"What do we do to get started?" Myerson asked. "I need to make progress fast."

"I'd like Hal Levinson to join Jane and myself for discussions with some of your staff in representative U.S. locations and with several of the overseas managers," replied Blake. "He knows the ropes from his own experience and together we can diagnose and verify the basic problems from these interviews.

Then I'd suggest scheduling a meeting with all your key managers who are involved in the problem."

"From all over the world? Review it for me again. What would we be doing?" queried Myerson.

"Basically, taking some simple, progressive steps toward positive change," said Blake. "First, agreement is reached among all the principals on the soundest basis for operating a worldwide trading company in a profitable and sound manner. Normally this can be achieved fairly readily, as thinking in ideal terms and from the perspective of the problem's internal logic facilitates arriving at an optimal solution. Next, the actual situation is described. Agreement here is not easy, but less difficult than you might think because descriptions can be based on specific instances and examples. Participants explore the situation's history, actively focusing on how and why relationships, practices, procedures, and so on have developed in certain ways and not in others. Achieving understanding and agreement in this area is critical to lasting cultural change. Finally, action plans are developed to overcome history and bridge the gap between the soundest and actual situations."

"With people from so many places involved, can we realistically expect to get all of them together on anything?" Myerson asked. "I've been here a long time, and I'm not even sure we could agree that black is black or white's white, and the tensions between headquarters and the field will be a major impediment to any progress."

"Finding objective solutions to a problem knows no nationality, and the organizational components involved do not constitute a barrier. Differences in attitudes and values can never be completely resolved, but they do not have to impede problem solving," Mouton noted. "Although there are differences in national sociology, there are no real differences in underlying human psychology and value systems. The same behavioral theories apply the world over. The multinational nature of your organization isn't an insurmountable barrier in gaining shared commitment to a global strategy."

"Is it really a good idea to be so open about things like this?"

questioned Myerson. "Won't it just result in arguments, accusations, resentment, and hostility and reopen old wounds? At best, what will we get besides good intentions, which may never materialize? We've had that already."

"The integration plan earns the commitment of everyone who participates in creating it, and motivation generated through the integration process translates good intentions into sound actions. There'll be disagreements, as there are now, but they can be resolved through openness and candor that permits differences to be confronted. Follow-up is then needed and *wanted*, but this is a strong beginning," said Blake.

"Well, look," said Myerson, "I don't want to be a damper or a wet blanket, but what are the risks in this kind of thing? That's what I want to know."

"The risks are of two types. Let me deal with each," Blake continued. "The first is no progress will be made. That in itself is not a genuine risk, but the *attitudes* associated with failure to make progress is a risk. Continuation into the future of the same problem can result in people becoming disheartened, discouraged, and feeling defeated. They may be even less ready in the future to make another attempt at a solution than they are at the present, and I take it there isn't even all that much enthusiasm right now. This is not to be minimized because the experience of failure can have the demoralizing effects I have described.

"The second potential risk is to the futures of individuals. In this kind of confrontation session, competencies become more apparent than they may be in one-to-one dealings, but the same goes for lack of competence. Incompetencies, too, are subject to public scrutiny, and the person who suffers from publicly unveiled incompetence is in a weaker position in the future than he or she may have been in the past. This use of the term is almost a misuse, however, because organizations do not exist to protect incompetence. They exist to use resources to the fullest. If a person's competence is above some significant minimum, administrative actions related to replacement are rarely considered. If competence is below that threshold, it probably is in the best interest of that person in the long term to find employment within his or her area of competence. It certainly is in the interest of the organization that it employ people who can solve problems, keep the organization viable and growing, and give security to the many."

"There is an associated risk here," Levinson added. "It's not related to competence but to integrity. There always is the possibility that individuals will have been dealing in an underhanded manner. We know that organizations are correctly characterized as political institutions as well as systems of accomplishment. If people have been dealt with in an underhanded or unfair way, or if practices of deception are tolerated, these qualities also are likely to come into public view. When they do, it can be unfortunate for the person whose behavior is exposed, but again, this is a risk that is by no means an unfair risk. Deception and Machiavellian ways of operating are destructive of the system in the first place, and bringing these into the light reduces the risks to organizational health that are associated with them."

"The gain to the organization is that managerial actions can be taken that reduce the likelihood of its recurrence," Mouton said. "This means a more open and authentic organization that is characterized by greater integrity. These are values that make for effective organizational problem solving rather than impede it. That's my assessment of the risks involved."

Lombard remarked, "If that constitutes an assessment of the risks, the only one of any concern to me is the consequences associated with failure to be successful. I understand that, and I appreciate your putting it in perspective, but it gives us another dilemma. Either we don't try for fear of failure, or we try and run the risk of failure. Which is better? Is it better to live with the status quo, which is less than satisfactory, or to risk an attempt to improve it and to fail?" Having asked the question, Lombard continued, "When I analyze the situation this way, I, for one, am ready for us to make a positive decision."

Diagnosing the Situation

After the decision to go ahead had been made, interviews were conducted with division managers from headquarters, regional operating locations, and a sample of international operations. Based on these discussions, Blake, Mouton, and Levinson discovered the core issues first-hand and became aware of tensions that surrounded them. Excerpts from these interviews give their flavor.

The View from Headquarters

Division headquarters is manned in the usual way with technical and staff groups giving background support. The key players are four "desk heads" roughly comparable with the more common corporate structures and a shipping director: Rodgers, cotton; Figueroa, wool; Swann, jute; Ames, flax, silk, and exotics; and Cally, traffic and shipping.

A group interview was conducted with these five key people. They were thirty-five to fifty-five years old, and only John Rodgers had not had field experience in the United States or Europe.

"Our biggest problem is that roles and responsibilities are unclear," explained Mark Swann.

"As I see it, we're intermediaries between operating locations and a market information clearing house," said Ames. "There are different markets, but all of them are interdependent, since they are interconnected in one way or another. This means that some centralization is needed to get the locations to play the same game by the same rules, or our size and diversity can work against us. Without order and predictability, it's a situation of prima donnas, each performing like a ballerina, each performing according to her own score."

"We don't have a crystal ball," Swann added, "so we usually just provide information and advice. Managers 'out there' generally make their own decisions."

Blake asked, "So what you are saying is that there are a number of strong components but without effective headquarters' direction and coordination?"

"That's it. We try to give directions, but they are not accepted. We seek to coordinate, but we have difficulties there, too," said Swann.

"We're also responsible for approving some contracts," said Maury Figueroa. "We put together all the information and prepare the paperwork because we have a broader perspective than any local office. You'd think the traders would appreciate the help, but they seem to think they could do better without us."

"Basically, we're running so hard that we lose track of where we are," said Jim Cally. "Each of us makes high-pressure decisions based on the situation and the person involved, not according to an intelligent, systematic master plan. Many of our efforts are shortsighted. They put out the latest fire, but don't prevent new ones."

"I want to get back to the issues of direction and coordination because that's where our problems seem to lie. What the others have said is true," agreed Swann. "As a result, we seem to operate on personalities, not policies. We're still looking for a direction. We'd have a rebellion if we put out stringent policy and guidelines; the field would see them as straightjackets. These are men of responsibility and pride. We can't afford to dictate to them, but we don't want to go back to the free-for-all of the last decade either. We need some middle ground," he concluded.

"In trying to pull this whole thing together," said Cally, "Myerson sometimes supports the idea of crystal-clear policies enforced by a strong headquarters. Other times, it's hands off. Sometimes we're like parole officers and other times we're strictly advisers. I think the field's even more confused by our inconsistency than we are."

"Our efforts to enforce established procedures are interpreted as centralized control, not direction and coordination," Figueroa added. "We need to clarify roles if we're ever going to go anywhere. But after all this time, I think we've come to tolerate and cope with ambiguity. As a matter of fact, I think the issue is not one of tolerating ambiguity, but of actively promoting it in the name of local option, decentralized decision making, and all the rest of it, which is justified under the traders' banner of 'wheel and deal.'"

"Maybe this meeting that's planned will help us get a better handle on things. At least we'll know better where we really stand," Ames remarked.

"What we've painted," said Rodgers, "is a pretty grim picture. If I were to summarize it, I'd say our comments add up to describing a headquarters that is not in control and a field that is out of control. It's a frightening situation. When you come right down to it, we are controlled by a world environment rather than being able to take actions that move us forward in a world environment. I think we've described the symptoms; personally, I don't feel that we've gotten down to explanations for why this situation is as it is. Having said that, don't ask me. I'm as baffled as anybody else."

Comments from U.S. Locations

The next visit was to several of Comtradco's offices in the United States, talking individually with Harris (Chicago), Thomas (Kansas City), Simpson (Houston), and Lewis (Portland)—the people who head the regional locations. Their comments focus primarily on headquarters' past performance. The following summaries of each interview are listed one after another to emphasize the recurrent themes:

Harris: I'm not sure they know what they're doing on the headquarters' desks. In fact, they don't even seem to know what they're supposed to do. The desk heads have had to cope with high turnover and their new people really haven't caught on yet. If a desk head is away—sick or on vacation—their staff is helpless.

Thomas: I know they're trying to be helpful, but more often than not they just slow us down. I work well with some headquarters' people, but most aren't responsive at all or they steer you the wrong way. I don't have time to put up with that nonsense just because procedure says I should. They complain I don't follow the rules, but my business and bonuses have held up well enough so far. I'm judged on my own profit/loss (P/L), and so long as that's the case, I'll do whatever I think is in my own best interest.

Simpson: Sometimes they help us put things together for a big contract. It's good to know their thinking on the markets even though I don't always agree. But in day-to-day operations they're less often a boon and more often a barrier. We almost lost my biggest contract of the year last month because it took so long to follow all the procedures. We've learned to work around them because it's so cumbersome to work with them.

Lewis: It's mostly a matter of individual personalities and abilities. Some in headquarters are okay but I have a huge problem with John Rodgers on the cotton desk. He's given me bad information, then tried to deny it, or blamed some new staff person. I pay as little attention to him as possible. Another problem with headquarters involves the big contracts they're responsible for. When everything works well and Myerson and Lombard are pleased, headquarters takes all the credit. If a deal starts to go sour, they suddenly lose interest and leave us to pick up the pieces. "Get into trouble together, get out of it alone" is the motto around here.

Perspective from Abroad

Two managers from abroad, Felipe Mitjana (Spain) and Enzo Barrani (Italy), provided a view of Comtradco's international locations. The discussion took place in Mitjana's Madrid office. In addition, the head man from Singapore was interviewed while he was visiting headquarters.

"I'm happy enough with the way we work with headquarters overall," Mitjana began. "Most of these people try hard, and the ones who've been around awhile are knowledgeable. Much of our trouble centers on two or three who are either incompetent or have so narrow an outlook that it has the same effect. I think they look at everything from a U.S. angle and don't understand our markets here in Europe. We have somewhat more flexibility than the U.S. locations do. We're far enough away to be pretty well left alone. This has always been a decentralized operation so we can take advantage of fast changes at the local level without long delays in getting approvals from afar."

"That's the point," said Barrani, the Italian trader. "They sit in headquarters, close to all that goes on in their own country, but all they know about Italy is pasta and Sophia Loren.

They're so myopic, they think Rome is only a city in upstate New York. I don't want them breathing down my neck, but I would appreciate some support once in awhile."

"Frankly," Mitjana suggested, "I think we could eliminate the headquarters desks altogether and get on just as well—maybe even better—without having to check with them for everything. I seem to spend as much time explaining to them what I need to do as it takes me to do it. I need more legitimate autonomy. Their so-called coordination sure isn't helping my bottom line."

"I've been in this organization for fifteen years, and the international locations are still treated like stepchildren," said Barrani. "I like the company overall or I'd go elsewhere. It's more than just nationality, it's a matter of consistency and objectivity, as well as knowledge and ability."

Mitjana agreed: "They know intellectually that things can't be done in all locations exactly as they're done in the home market, but they labor over every exception, so that it's preferable to inform them after the fact of what you've done—not to ask them beforehand. There *are* good reasons for some variations, but they filter everything through that big American lens and don't want to see something different. If consistency is the hobgoblin of small minds, the New York gang has got to be a bunch of pinheads. They worship it as an intrinsic value rather than a framework from which deviations that move the company forward are encouraged. What they regard as consistency we see as rigidity."

"Let me give you an example," Barrani interrupted. "Hans Mueller from Geneva has worked two years to open some new markets for us in Iraq and Sudan. It takes a lot of time and flexibility, and the U.S. headquarters desk is uncomfortable with anything that's 'different.' They want the kind of quick simple business that they've always had. Next month's meeting will be a good chance for them to get to know us. I'm not sure we can honestly expect much more from it. Companies like ours seem committed to maintaining the status quo. It's a matter of evolution. We'd even make Darwin impatient."

Releasing the Hold of History

Twenty-four managers were nominated for the Phase 3 activity. This all took place within six weeks of Julian Lombard's pronouncement that "something drastic must be done." Participating managers were organized into three groups: headquarters (including Myerson), U.S. regional locations, and international locations.

At the first joint session, each group was seated at its own table in the large central conference room. Blake, Mouton, and Levinson introduced the meeting and quickly called attention to the importance of the three groups reaching agreement on the soundest model for operating the world trade division. The model would provide a framework for organizing divisional resources so that all parts of the operation would fit together.

"In our interviews with you, the question of how centralized or decentralized you ideally would be emerged as a critical issue," Blake began. "We propose this issue to serve as a point of departure and suggest that an ideal position for integrating this organization be developed around it. A sound beginning is to list all the *elements* that are essential to the interface between headquarters and the field locations if the business is to be conducted in the soundest manner. Then, for each element, describe the optimal basis for interaction."

"How idealistic can we be?" asked Jim Cally from the headquarters table.

"The first step is to develop a model of excellence," Mouton said, "without regard for the past. If you could make the relationship a perfect one from your standpoint, what would it be like? If it sounds general or abstract, try to make it concrete with examples and illustrations. Later on we'll add further specifics so that everyone knows what the generalizations are intended to mean in operational terms."

Designing an Optimal Model for Headquarters-Field Integration

Following several hours of discussion in separate rooms, the groups reconvened to share the three models of the soundest relationship between headquarters and operating locations. A spokesperson for the U.S. locations began by presenting charts describing the model they had produced. International and then headquarters followed with explanations of the elements in their soundest relationship models. Spokespersons representing the other two groups asked questions for clarification. After the U.S. and international locations consolidated their perceptions, agreement was reached between the field and corporate descriptions.

The U.S. and international locations had the same general feeling for what a sound relationship with headquarters would be, but they were by no means identical. The U.S. locations felt that they tend to be oversupervised and foreign locations felt ignored. Thus the U.S. locations had a better perspective on how headquarters viewed global operations than was true for foreign locations, each of which had come to think of itself as an isolated profit center. One might offer a helping hand to another center, but only when there was little or nothing to lose. As the broader issues of global integration came into view, both foreign and domestic locations saw that a local action might be needed that was detrimental to that location but advantageous to the corporation as a whole. A corporate perspective was preferable to and sounder than that of a regional location.

Thus the issue turned not on what perspective should be employed but rather on establishing a sound reward system for taking a corporate perspective rather than a local one. After the list was consolidated, the next step involved a general session for reviewing the list and questions of clarification regarding the next steps.

"It's hard to believe," observed Myerson, "that we've come up with the sort of things I've been trying to get us to grapple with for years, and we've done it ourselves as a team effort."

"I'm really astonished," said Cally from headquarters.

"Same here," agreed Lewis from Portland. "Our group is especially surprised to see how much importance we all place on mutual trust and respect. Our group feels it's really a pivotal issue, and the degree of emphasis we've placed on it must be indicative of the work to be done. Frankly, we never expected headquarters to say that they'd trust each of us to do a good job."

"We have the same reaction to headquarters' sound statement about domestic and international markets," said Felipe Mitjana. "We're still somewhat skeptical, but international is very encouraged that headquarters recognizes and is concerned about eliminating the U.S. bias."

After spirited discussion of the meanings and implications of the various elements, Barrani (Italy) brought the discussion toward a conclusion, "I subscribe to what you have up there. Give us the answers to those questions and we'll leave two days early and get back to making money."

Harris (Chicago) added, "Those elements are about as big and basic as the paragraphs in the American Constitution."

"It might be hard to restrain ourselves," said Thomas (Kansas City), "but let's try to leave it alone and not add anymore, because if we do, pretty soon we'll have a twenty-first amendment, a twenty-second amendment, and then a thousand interpretative rulings on what we meant to say in those five. We have the spirit of what's trying to be accomplished. That's what's important. If we understand one another's intentions, we're halfway home. I'd like to ask that we accept it as it is now written and move forward. Could we?"

Levinson reentered the discussion by asking, "Are there further questions? If not, let's take the model as produced to represent a tentative statement and see how well we can work with it. It's a sound basis for making progress in strengthening the development of direction and coordination throughout the system."

"Traders buying in to the concept of a corporate orientation is like a dream come true," quipped Myerson. "If there wasn't so much to be done before the sound model can become an actuality, I'd suggest we all go home."

"We're just getting our Fiat out of first gear," Barrani concluded. "Now that there's a model that we all agree represents excellence in our relationship, we can look at what we really do by comparison. Our sound model represents a challenge to which we're all committed. I'm anxious to move forward."

Exploring Actual Conditions

For the next activity, the groups were asked to describe actual conditions for the first element, "Corporate Orientation." As part of this task, they identified historical events that might explain current conditions.

Corporate Orientation Versus Emphasis on Local P/L

Following separate discussions, each group presented its perceptions of actual circumstances surrounding corporate orientation through spokespersons. Discussions centered on the appropriate importance to place on local P/L in evaluating performance and determining bonuses.

"The corporation's best interest is certainly what we emphasize, at least in principle," said Barrani, "but let's admit that the system doesn't reward or reinforce that principle. Headquarters wants and recognizes an entrepreneurial, competitive attitude, and that's the way it's always been. I'm responsible for the Italian P/L and my bonus every year is based on what I can produce."

"That might have been true before," Cally, spokesperson for the headquarters group, admitted, "but not any longer. Our priority is overall company results—and has been since the division was formed. Emphasis on local P/L's is a vestige of the past."

Lewis, representing the U.S. locations, objected strongly. "Maybe you'd like to think things have changed, but the evidence says otherwise. Just last month Myerson was really upset with me for my big profit drop last quarter. I acted in the corporate interest and transferred an order to Los Angeles for a better delivery schedule, and all I got for being such a nice guy was a hard time."

"And what about Griffith's predecessor in Singapore?" added Barrani. "Everyone knows he served this company well for many years, but when his local P/L went down to break-even two years ago, he got shafted. Even though he made substantial contributions to overall profit, you were all disappointed with his individual results. Now he's gone. No matter what you'd like to think, out in the field all that counts is looking out for number one."

"It's not that we're disloyal," said Lewis (Portland). "We all know how important corporate profit is to the health of our individual operations. We're just asking that the reward system encourage a corporate orientation rather than discourage it."

"And when headquarters evaluates a trader's performance," reminded Barrani, "we'd appreciate your being consistent with what you say about corporate versus local interests. In other words, practice what you preach. In the field what we see is a headquarters that operates by a double standard. When a P/L is unfavorable, we catch hell for that. When we resist entering into a contract that will make the other guy look good and us bad, we catch hell for that. See what we're saying? You can't hold us responsible on a P/L level and ask us to sacrifice business in the corporate interest at the same time. Play it one way or play it the other, but you can't do both. As long as headquarters is not prepared to act according to a single set of criteria, this confusion, lack of coordination, and contradiction will continue. To capture it all in a word, 'chaos' prevails. Another way of saying it is that 'cut-throat' competition between commodity traders takes priority over coherent cooperation."

"Barrani," said Myerson, "you may have trouble spelling, but you sure can alliterate!"

"Okay," responded Cally. "I can't argue with the weight of evidence you've presented. Historically, I have to say we've been inconsistent, but we're committed to making whatever policy and procedural changes are needed to ensure that things are different in the future."

"Right," added Myerson. "Now that we've surfaced old resentments and frustrations, maybe we can focus not on how things have been, but on how they might be. We'll all ultimately benefit from the changes you've requested and we endorse.

In order to solve this double standard, we need to create a strong reward system consistent with supporting corporate P/L."

Trust and Respect

Trust and respect was the second element considered. The trading groups agreed that many of headquarters' policies and procedures were unnecessary, given the high degree of competence and professionalism demonstrated at both the U.S. and international locations. Headquarters countered that the traders did not appreciate or value their expertise and their efforts to encourage traders to get the best deals when considered from a corporate point of view. They felt that their attempts to be helpful were often seen as interference.

In addition, much of the discussion circled around the trust and respect problem until it reached individual persons and their contributions or lack thereof. One example of candor emerged during the trust and respect exchange when the U.S. traders pointed to specific instances where Figueroa had shown personal bias in determining the fair market price at which goods would be sold from one region to another.

Another example involved Rodgers and the traders' perception that he refused to take responsibility by covering up his mistakes, often placing blame on another staff member or on the locations. Rodgers twisted in his chair when Myerson asked for specific instances. The U.S. traders cited several in which Rodgers failed to do his job properly and then refused to admit it.

Barrani made a similar generalization from international's perspective, stating, "There is also one major exception to the trust and respect we hold for headquarters staff, but we don't believe that a meeting like this provides a proper forum for discussing individuals. We're all agreed on this," he said, looking to other members of his group for support.

"But it doesn't help to say you don't have trust if you don't provide facts," said Myerson angrily.

"We just don't think it's right to point fingers in public," Barrani replied. Several members of his group nodded to confirm their agreement. "We'll take care of it in our own way, privately and quietly. That's the only gentlemanly thing to do."

The room fell silent. One could suddenly hear the sound of fresh air circulating and muffled sounds from the hallway. After a lengthy silence, Blake remarked, "It seems we have an example here from which we can learn something about openness and candor. The key point is whether or not international's approach is consistent with honesty and forthrightness. Is it truly 'gentlemanly' or helpful to suppress or sublimate conflict? Does reluctance to confront these issues reflect trust and respect or doubt and suspicion?"

"Each group will choose a course of action it feels is appropriate," added Levinson, "but the choice has consequences in terms of others' reactions. Openness elicits greater openness, repression results in greater withholding. The best way to ensure that others will be honest and forthright is to set the example. Withholding troublesome information encourages others to be less than candid in return. Relationships suffer, to say nothing of the costliness of failed decisions to the corporation."

The subject of trust and respect was concluded in the first few minutes of the next morning's general session. John Rodgers stood up the moment the room had quieted.

"You probably already know that international was talking about me last night. Their complaints were essentially the same as those that the U.S. group spoke about. It involves the accusation about my covering up mistakes and shifting the responsibility for them to others. I'm committed to seeing that this doesn't happen again, and if I backslide, please let *me* know so I can make immediate corrections."

Everyone listened thoughtfully, somewhat skeptical yet hopeful that public acknowledgment and Rodgers's evident "change of heart" and invitation to challenge any relapses would move him in the direction of solving a basic problem.

Global Perspective Versus Location Perspective

Once this level of trust and respect was present, discussion of the global strategy surfaced and several issues and problems could then be publicly analyzed and resolved in a way that brought forward the full complexity and subtlety of issues necessary for finding creative solutions.

Generally, headquarters admitted its need to work more closely with the international locations and to rely more heavily on traders' first-hand knowledge of regional, political, and economic conditions. Examples were cited wherein headquarters had erroneously assumed an "expert" orientation and, without the latest information and operating from its own remote location, had provided faulty advice. Conversely, either feeling they would not be listened to or out of apathy, locations acknowledged that they had failed to keep headquarters well informed of important national developments. Improved communication was clearly needed for traders to have access to important information and for headquarters to make intelligent, informed recommendations, particularly as they related to cooperation in the corporate interests among locations.

Specifically, pros and cons of developing a market with China were reviewed. Griffith (Singapore) explained the enormity of the potential. "For some of our basic fibers," he said, "the ultimate potential could be more than 10 percent of our current worldwide sales. We can also develop a huge quality source of supply, particularly in silk and other exotics, but we'll have to make a substantial investment and offer at least a 5 percent discount. Locating and securing supply sources will require frequent contacts and visits, and I think we should get started there before our competitors. Singapore provides us a window into China and it's a key listening post for all of southeast Asia. If it's in the corporate interest, I would be willing to take initiative to do so, but I would need headquarters' support in terms of a whole new way of looking at the Asian business."

"That sounds right to me," agreed Myerson, "and it reflects the global corporate perspective we need. If your local P/L falls off while you concentrate on this key piece of business, others need to take up the slack. Headquarters needs to adapt to facilitate this and other corporate-oriented initiatives. The days of just counting the cash register at the end of every month have got to stop. We're building for the future."

"But look at what you've just said, Joel," exclaimed Griffith. "You've just spoken the double standard again. In one breath you say local P/L and in the next 'building for the future.' This is our problem. You want it both ways. You want to judge us on cash register earnings and then you want us to take actions that impact adversely on short-term profits. The only solution that I can imagine for this kind of thing is that we move in the direction of an MBO orientation. Joel, you and I can do an in-depth study for the prospects of southeast Asia and southern China, and we can also look at swap-out opportunities that arise for the Singapore office when we have contracts for Australia, Indonesia, and Thailand. I tell you my best estimate of profit and loss for whatever length of time reasonable stability can be assumed in the context of developing the China trade, and so on. You provide your inputs of what you expect of me based on the possible swing deals that headquarters may be able to create with Singapore as one of the principals.

"Once we hash that all out," Griffith continued, "that becomes my MBO contract with Comtradco, and I would expect you to judge my performance in the light of its terms corrected for unforeseeable eventualities like political uneasiness in southeast Asia. Then you'd be judging me against a jointly developed plan, Joel, not against some numbers at the bottom of a page and not against some subjective judgment of the adverse effect on corporate P/L from trying to penetrate the China trade. If we could do this, and all of the other major traders as well, it would provide you deeper insights into our operating problems and opportunities and give us greater confidence in headquarters' contracts and deals."

"Well, it sounds to me as though it would stop this swing between local P/L and corporate interests," responded Myerson. "What do others of you think?"

"And that would mean that from now on, no more complaints about the Iraqi venture," exulted Mueller. "Nobody else would touch that business, and it's taken a huge amount of work on my part. Even though headquarters thought the effort was unjustified, it looks now as though it's paying off. If the whole place doesn't blow up, we'll be number one for years in a market that neither we nor our competitors have been able to penetrate before." He looked intently at Rodgers who grinned and raised a thumb.

"Sudan is another good example," Myerson noted. "They, too, have unique requirements like special terms, different delivery guarantees, extended payment schedules, and so on. I suppose progress there requires additional departures from standardized ways of doing business."

"I'm really beginning to understand," said Rodgers. "The trouble is that these out-of-the-ordinary efforts take so much time and seem unnecessarily complicated. Now that I know the background I can see that conventional approaches won't work. I'll be giving this kind of activity more attention in the future. It can really make the difference for us if we're successful in these areas."

The discussion of the actual issues continued, centering on the fundamental issues already identified: corporate orientation versus location perspective as the basis for business decisions, the impact of performance appraisal, incentive compensation programs, undertaking new market development and absorbing the expense locally, and the distortions of performance related to uncontrollable factors such as border closings and unavailability of transportation.

After completing the consolidation of the actual description, Myerson summarized his conclusions and perspective on the next steps. "We've always needed this clarity and agreement, but I thought it was still years away. Now I see that many of the barriers were here at home—in the headquarters group, generally, and in my own leadership, specifically. I think our first step should be to identify specific actions we need to take for headquarters to improve its operation and exercise real strategic leadership and then for the locations to strengthen and modify their efforts. Next, there are specific things we need to do together to get our relationship straightened out. I'll take personal responsibility for investigating how to bring a reward system into place that recognizes the contribution to corporate P/L that locations contribute. I will have recommendations to present to you within the next two months. This will give us time to set plans in motion and to iron out the bugs in what needs to be done based on the work we'll finish here."

Planning for Change

When the session was opened for consideration of specific steps, the groups were restructured to include proportionate representation from headquarters, the U.S. locations, and the international locations. This reinforced the need for collaboration among those present.

Four groups responded to the following task question for this activity: "What specific steps can be taken on the authority of those present, by whom, by when, to achieve what specific results?" Every group discussed the "trust and respect" element and one of the other four elements. The newly structured groups formulated specific plans and then presented and critiqued them in a general session. Activities, timetables, and assignments of responsibility were clearly established and specific follow-up steps were outlined.

"To wrap the session up," said Myerson, "I'm not here to pronounce a benediction, but I would like to place what we have accomplished in perspective. Our division has not done well for the past three years. I suspect it is reasonably widely known among you that Julian Lombard has been concerned that the actions we have taken haven't brought about the turnaround that's needed for long-term health. He was dubious about this meeting, but he asked me to probe possibilities with Hal Levinson. Hal put us on the track that we've been through.

"I can now tell you with confidence that I am prepared to go to Lombard and report that in my view—and, speaking for what I've heard others say, from your perspective, too—we now have the framework for lifting ourselves by the bootstraps. We have a commitment to take actions to bring about what we want to occur. These have been intense days. I realize that many of you have come a great distance. This meeting is another interruption of your family lives. There's no way to correct for this, but there is one way of acknowledging it. I want to express my personal appreciation for the efforts made here."

"Speaking for the group," said Barrani, "you have our support for talking to Julian Lombard as you have said you will. I now suggest that we break."

Dynamics of Change

Comtradco's shift away from individualized, vested interests to a global, corporate orientation illustrates the dynamics of change described in earlier chapters. By analyzing the intervention in these terms, change is clearly seen as a dynamic process, not an isolated event of dealing with individuals, one after another.

Influence of History

A negative history was at the core of conflict in the headquarters-field relationship at Comtradco. Initially, historical perceptions and misperceptions continued to block progress and impede change. As history was explored, analyzed, and positively dealt with during the development session, change became a viable possibility and eventual reality.

Headquarters had developed a view of the field as unappreciative, disrespectful, sometimes devious, and often uncooperative. Examples of perceived resistance to headquarters' attempts to provide guidance and direction (headquarters' perception) or to exercise control (field's perception) reinforced this opinion. At headquarters, the field was seen as a group of freewheeling entrepreneurs, willing to sacrifice the corporation to achieve its own objectives. Members of the headquarters group began the interface development session convinced that nothing short of a miracle could generate field commitment to the greater corporate good.

Both field groups held similarly negative perceptions of headquarters as incompetent, inconsistent, too bureaucratic, and overcontrolling. Their arsenal of complaints was loaded with historical instances of perceived injustices and inequities. As their initial comments and behavior illustrate, the field obviously held little hope for constructive attitudinal and behavioral change.

Since history was shielding cooperative, collaborative alternatives from view, strategies for coping with poor interface relationships failed to surface and conflict was masked. Headquarters managed as best it could by dealing with each location on an individual basis rather than as part of an integrated whole. To avoid open conflict, managers learned what individual locations would or would not tolerate and adapted their behavior accordingly.

Likewise, the field learned which headquarters people to trust and which to avoid. The field became expert in evading established procedures, short-circuiting requirements, and circumventing channels. The rule was to get by and to accept mediocre relationships and results as unchangeable, if not inevitable.

Modeling Excellence

With the model of a sound relationship embraced as a standard of excellence, the groups no longer accepted poor interface relationships, but strived instead to optimize their interaction and results.

Commitment to a superordinate goal, that is, implementing a corporate orientation, and the kind of motivation required to achieve it are an integral component of this intervention's success. The turning point occurred when both headquarters and field came to recognize how strongly they believed in the same things—trust, respect, a sound corporate strategy, and a global business perspective. Once a basis for agreement became self-evident, the goal of corporate profitability received broad endorsement. "How to's" were readily resolved in the climate of mutual trust and respect, which developed when these groups realized they ultimately wanted and needed the same things.

Beyond the specific accomplishments that flowed from this conference, the stage was set for a much longer range and sounder approach to organizational success by linking such organization development goals as mutual trust and respect and corporate orientation to a reward system tied to corporate profitability rather than to incentives that were entirely dependent on local performance.

Shared Objectivity

Shared objectivity was achieved by the thorough probing of history, which produced agreement on what had been and what needed to be changed. Progress was made when each group could recognize its past actions that had led to problems and its unwitting role in preventing their solution. Myerson's comment, "Now I see that many of the barriers were here at home—in the headquarters group, generally, and in my own leadership, specifically," represents the level of perceptual objectivity achieved.

Membership Norm Shifting

No individual member was forced to risk negative sanctions by changing from a group-held position in isolation. Group members had the opportunity to think through and evaluate alternative behavior patterns and new attitudes collectively, so that change could occur in the entire group simultaneously. As they became aware of the unsatisfactory norms controlling their behavior, headquarters and field reached consensual decisions to forsake the past and pursue a sounder future.

Group discussions of problems included exposing and dealing with specific past transgressions, presenting opposing viewpoints candidly, and facing personally ineffective and inappropriate behavior. The field's reactions to Rodgers's perceived incompetence demonstrated the potentially positive effects of candor and confrontation. Rodgers's acknowledgment of responsibility generated a sympathetic feeling toward him even though he had violated norms of integrity, and it resulted in others extending credibility to him for his readiness to be forthright. This is fundamental in rebuilding trust.

Centralization/Decentralization

The Comtradco interface was a vertical relationship among the headquarters and the other two groups; headquarters' power over the other two put it in a position to mandate a solution on the basis of coercion, if nothing else. As the study demonstrates, headquarters was able to suspend reliance on power and authority for dealing with the problem while the field locations were able to deal with the higher level organization in an open way, devoid of politics. The field locations also embraced a corporate orientation once it became clear that each of the field representatives was prepared to commit to one another a mutual obligation to act according to the same standards of decision making. This mutual obligation was the basis for shared confidence that equitable treatment by headquarters would be based on overall contribution rather than on looking good in the local context only.

The Issue of Centralization/Decentralization

Any complex organization with local P/L accountability is likely to encounter the problems that prevented Comtradco from increasing its corporate P/L. A subordinate organization may act against corporate interests when it decides a problem in terms favorable to local profit and loss. The problem is exaggerated when headquarters rewards a subordinate component based on P/L, even while denying that it is influencing its own judgments. As a result, a major dilemma facing executives today involves securing commitment to a global corporate strategy from operating managers in all parts of the world. As organizations expand beyond national boundaries, a healthy interface between headquarters and field locations is critical for mutually supportive efforts in pursuit of corporate goals. Neither centralization nor decentralization offers an optimally effective approach to needed cooperation and collaboration if these run counter to the exercise of sound judgment or the advancement and/or protection of vested interests.

When an organization has worldwide concerns, centralization is perhaps impossible and certainly impractical. Managers in the field need flexibility and adaptability to respond to changing political, social, and economic conditions. Headquarters is typically at a disadvantage in terms of detailed information or current perspectives on global developments. Field managers are in positions to have the maximum amount of pertinent data. Since they are also responsible for implementation, headquarters' intervention into the decision-making process may be regarded as interfering, or even inappropriate.

Decentralization is not an entirely attractive alternative. Effective use of available corporate resources demands some degree of centralized decision making, budgeting, accounting, supervision, and development of senior personnel. Achieving corporate objectives requires concerted effort in a deliberate direction according to an agreed-on master plan. Every separate field location is a component of the large corporate puzzle and must interlock with others to complete the picture.

Since both centralization and decentralization offer problematic answers to how best to manage a global organization, many executives search for a third alternative, some middle ground that provides a balance. In some organizations, the pendulum swings back and forth between the two extremes. When either is practiced

for awhile and becomes untenable, the other appears more acceptable, is adopted, and the cycle repeats itself.

The intervention reported here illustrates *integration*. This
can prove to be an effective way to coordinate geographically dis-
persed operations, enhance commitment to a global strategy, and
ensure cooperative effort in their achievement. Integration is not a
compromise between centralization and decentralization. Instead,
it describes a process of participation and involvement applied between the corporate level and division components in a way that
brings motivation and attitudes into congruence with the requisite
problem-solving structure for maximizing gain. The same process
occurs in smaller organizations at the department or division level.

Integration can occur when headquarters and field locations
jointly outline a corporate strategy in global terms and design a
structure for implementing it on a continuing basis. With this model
providing guidance and direction, interdependent action replaces
independence and dependence, or imposition and resistance.
Separate entities can then clearly understand their contribution to
corporate results and expect and receive headquarters' encourage-
ment as well as agreed-on support. Neither side holds the upper hand
because the headquarters-field relationship is based on trust and
respect rather than power and authority or abdication.

Conclusion

Looking at this intervention from three years later, steady
progress has been made toward improved organizational integration. With an exception or two, the corporate orientation has been
factored into local decisions and the reward structure changed so
that the incentive compensation is based on corporate contribution.
An equitably administered compensation program has reinforced
reliance on the corporate orientation in local decision making.

Application in Cockpit and Medical Arenas

Not all situations present the kind of problem with which this
chapter has been concerned. For example, cockpit crews look to the
union as their representative in dealing with management, but the
problem per se is not one that can be worked out between crews and
management directly. On the other hand, it represents a very
natural opportunity to relieve tensions that crew members experience toward the management of the company through an or-

ganized approach in which union leaders and corporate representatives engage in collaborative problem solving.

By comparison, the field of medicine is liberally populated with interface problems, both at the professional level and between the professional level and administrative personnel. Some of these interface difficulties are between the doctors as medical professionals and nurses as the support system. Other similar conflicts exist between medical groups and the laboratory personnel, between nurses and the dietary and food service operation, and so on. It is unnecessary to go further as the point has been made. Medical institutions have only begun to come to terms with the intense interface conflicts developing within them. Some will take years to bring under resolution. Perhaps the most pressing at the present time involves the doctor/nurse interface, and this is only recently being examined. It involves engaging nurses in Medical Grid Seminars. At a certain point in the sequence, however, the nursing staff is segregated from the medical group and the two undergo the six-step model presented earlier.

In another example, we were invited to do an organization diagnosis in a major American hospital. Apart from personal and within-team problems that sometimes surface when undertaking such an activity, we encounter issues of intergroup conflict. Various groups within the organization or with which the organization interacts are at loggerheads with one another. This case was no different. Several examples of underlying tensions were revealed to us in interviews that were conducted at all levels throughout the hospital. Some of the initial problems identified were as follows:

1. *Lack of common goals:*
   - Doctors don't want to care for unexciting patients; surgical and medical doctors won't give up beds to one another.
   - Lab won't adjust fees to keep business in hospital.
   - Social workers/nurses/pharmacy question doctors about medical dosage.
   - No one knows if teaching or service is our primary goal.

2. *Unclear communication:*
   - Blood tests approved without notifying accounting or pharmacy.
   - Memos don't get to all the right people.

- Patients admitted without checking if beds available.
- Lines of responsibility unclear.

3. *Lack of clear coordination:*
   - Patient care not coordinated between medical students, social workers, and nurses; this results in duplication of effort and needless inquiry.
   - Patients should be given prescriptions for medication when discharged but doctors give them free samples beforehand, and we can't control the dosage.
   - A responsible party, e.g., accounting, not getting required information with result that another group, e.g., pharmacy, has to search it out.

4. *Leadership:*
   - Power struggle between administration and accounting regarding who "owns" the hospital.
   - Pertinent information not passed on to responsible professional people who could facilitate the process.
   - Sense of urgency conveyed without any facts.
   - Rumored dishonesty within management.
   - Leadership operates on crisis management basis; lack of trust at lower levels regarding this Grid development effort due to past history.

5. *Atmosphere:*
   - Fluctuates between being paternalistic toward employees and an "I don't give a damn" attitude.
   - In group meetings management looks for opportunity to "catch employees and get them."

6. *Staffing:*
   - Overqualified personnel staff certain positions that could be filled by less expensive person.
   - Starting new program with little or no thought as to provisions for staffing.

7. *Cost consciousness:*
   - Difference in commitment level.
   - Lacks honest appraisal of priorities, hard work put into budget and then no further communication ever received by levels below.

As a result of observations gleaned from the interviews, representatives of the different groups involved congregated for purposes of a multiple intergroup activity using the Interface Conflict-Solving Model. Discussion took place to identify key barriers and possible solutions, with members coming to consensus on realistic action steps to deal with each of the problems and to earn commitment to their implementation. A sample of some of these barriers and solutions is listed as follows:

Communications

Barriers

Programs and projects that affect ancillary operations are initiated without prior announcement. Meetings often purposeless, summarily canceled, and/or unstructured. Supervisors often ignorant of facts because they do not have information and procedures and/or receive incomplete distribution of revised policies.

Solutions

Comprehensive distribution of directives, memos, and announcements that affect hospital operations. Better administrative manual. Pertinent agenda of current hospital topics.

Decision Making

Barriers

"Cart before the horse" syndrome, where "masterminding" occurs after the decision has been made. The lack of planning tends to generate mistakes that are perpetuated.

Solutions

Creation of a planning process that incorporates the thinking of all the individuals with a stake in the outcomes.

The New Business Environment

Barriers

The impression remains that hospitals are somehow removed from the impact of prevailing economic realities. The existent attitude among

Solutions

Accurate and current departmental budget reports. An information campaign throughout the hospital to make people aware of economic all levels of employees is that supplies are available in unlimited quantities. Excessive misutilization of same is the result.

conditions as they touch the hospital and its resources.

Responsibilities

Barriers

Unclear delineation of responsibility for a particular activity. Different departments getting a piece of the same action; overlapping. Departments tend to insulate themselves from shared responsibilities that they have in common with other departments—creating a win/lose situation.

Solutions

Better definition of departmental objectives and responsibilities that are easily understood and not left to subjective interpretation. Where possible, integrating similar activities into one whole.

Standards

Barriers

No uniform standards throughout the institution in applying personnel policies. Reporting of departmental progress and problems is mainly verbal and therefore the only control is defined by the shibboleth of past practices, e.g., Dr. X takes his secretary to lunch for two hours.

Solutions

Promulgation of standards that can be uniformly interpreted and applied by the hospital's departments.

Conflict

Barriers

Conflict between individuals and departments tends to be addressed on the basis of personality and is not approached as an organizational problem.

Solutions

More Grids!

Control

Barriers	Solutions
Individual departments function in a vacuum, e.g., nursing is like a mushroom with all the controls—penetrating agreement, etc., settled and remaining at the top. Each department has its own way of getting things done.	Education of all, and adherence to uniform hospital policies.

The preceding list demonstrates a number of serious intergroup problems. Through use of the Interface Conflict-Solving Model, many have gained greater definition. Solutions are in place for implementation and follow through.

Summary

In conclusion, ten key properties make up the design of the Interface Conflict-Solving Model.

1. Active participation by those on either side of the cleavage whose understanding and agreement are essential to support any change.

2. The ability of those who have the problem to learn to diagnose its causes.

3. Reliance on active participation by members to develop the insights, understandings, and agreements that serve as the basis for problem solving rather than using coercion, compromise, or capitulation.

4. The description of a complex intergroup relationship in terms of elements.

5. The proposition that *ideal* formulations can be composed and agreed to regarding the soundest relationship between them.

6. The identification of the status for these same elements in regard to the actual relationship.

7. The achievement of mutual agreement reflecting consolidation of viewpoints across groups.

8. The creation of discrepancies with resultant motivations to close the gap by comparing ideal with actual.

9. An interaction between groups that is carried out by spokespersons rather than by designated leaders. Shared understanding promoted by everyone involved in the relationship studying the situation and how to change it at the same time.

10. A structure and sequencing that permits a line or staff person to implement the process without being actively involved in the content of the activity itself.

By the time Intergroup Development activities of Phase 3 are completed, five major follow-up applications of Grid learning to real work problems have been made.

1. Every manager has acquired an understanding of theories of managerial behavior useful in mobilizing human energies around corporate purposes of profitability.

2. Application projects (Phase 1A) have been undertaken to revise norms adverse to productivity.

3. Every boss has studied, evaluated, and had the opportunity to strengthen the quality of supervision as applied in specific work situations that have direct operational consequences.

4. Every organized team where people need to join efforts to get synergistic results has been studied and evaluated. Each team has had the opportunity to strengthen the quality and character of its teamwork by moving away from historical ways of doing things toward strategies of work calculated to solve barriers to organization effectiveness.

5. Intergroup situations calling for cooperation and coordination have been studied and evaluated. Those responsible for each situation have had the opportunity to strengthen the quality and character of their coordinating efforts to achieve corporate aims.

With the completion of Phase 3, the behavioral dynamics that are embedded within the company's culture have been subjected to penetrating scrutiny. Nothing has been taken for granted. Rather, everything important that people do has been examined against models of excellence. Gaps have been identified. Specific projects, programs, and plans have been laid to help each individual, every team, and all interworking groups to change the situation from where it is to what it should be.

Reference

1. Blake, R. R., and J. S. Mouton. 1984. *Solving Costly Organizational Conflicts*. San Francisco: Jossey-Bass.

9

Developing the Operational
Side of the Business

Corporate leadership has by this time invested much energy in solving problems of the organization as a result of the learning and application activities of Phases 1 through 3. Many steps have already been taken to increase effectiveness by correcting current operating practices that are deficient and by strengthening those that are sound.

Fullest effectiveness, however, can be achieved only when attention is focused on the corporation's business culture, including its fundamental precepts, attitudes, beliefs, and values as they relate to the firm's business logic. The validity of these precepts, attitudes, beliefs, and values needs to be tested to ensure that the most rigorous thinking possible is being employed. Unless this is done, basic operational problems may persist that resist solution until the corporate strategy on which fundamental decisions are made is brought to greatest organization strength.

For purposes of analyzing and perfecting business logic, the firm as it has been known is set aside. The Ideal Strategic Corporate Model deals with fundamentals. The overall aim is to ensure that the basic strategies of the organization are "right." It provides a durable foundation for a sound, profitable, and growing organization that can be successful even under the most severe pressures of business cycles, competition, and rapid technological change. When completed, the strategic model may resemble the existing business system in varying degrees or it may differ radically. In any event, the strategic model is not to be viewed as fixed and unchangeable. It too is subject to modification, redefinition, and refinement as unforeseen and foreseeable conditions present themselves.

With the completion of Phase 4, Ideal Strategic Corporate Modeling, the organization has available a comprehensive set of business strategies to guide its growth and development. Without a strategic model, the existing corporate situation is likely to be taken for granted. Simply viewing obstacles as they are defined within the status quo may obscure more basic issues that lie beneath them but fail to be recognized as significant. Without a comprehensive strategy, much executive time is likely to be applied to dealing with issues that arouse interest, to eliminating difficulties that are irritating, or to coping with problems that appear urgent. In each case, executive action may be centered on short-term problem solving. As a result, solutions to these kinds of problems may be based on shallow business logic. The difficulties dealt with are not necessarily *basic*, but in the absence of a strategy that defines deeper lying concepts and issues of business, there is little option but to continue concentrating on superficial symptoms. A well-designed Ideal Strategic Corporate Model greatly increases the possibility that fundamental issues that need to be met will receive the attention they merit. These are likely to be issues that are critical to future corporate success when viewed over the long term.

Six Elements of Corporate Strategy

The Ideal Strategic Corporate Model encompasses six major elements. Top team members are asked to evaluate their corporation as they read through each element of corporate strategy. Assessment of the elements is to be in terms of each person's own understanding of an element as it currently exists within his or her firm. These judgments are designed to help corporate team members interpret the Phase 4 activity in the light of existing practices. The six elements include:

1. *Establishing Key Financial Objectives:* Corporate leadership has committed itself to achieving certain key financial objectives. Ideally these objectives are specified as minimum and optimum rates of return expected on investment employed and are expressed over a specific time period. In businesses where capital investment is a minor

factor and a poor index of corporate business effectiveness, financial objectives may be expressed as profit on sales or some alternative index of effectiveness. Service corporations and nonindustrial organizations such as government agencies do not have such an index but often do have or can develop quantitative indexes that are equally useful for measuring organization achievement.

2. *Defining the Nature of the Business(es):* A statement of the nature of the business(es) to which a company is committed is a vital aspect of the model. Of the almost infinite variety of possible business activities, best-fitting combinations and concentrations can be found. These are likely to be business activities that can yield both cumulative and synergistic results.

3. *Identifying the Nature of the Market(s):* The nature of the market is connected to the nature of the business. For analytical purposes, it often is important to treat these two elements as separate and distinct. Analyzing the nature of the business involves products or services from a manufacturing or production orientation, whereas analyzing the nature of the market emphasizes the selling or customer orientation. These two elements should be viewed both as separate aspects and as interdependent functions in the Ideal Strategic Corporate Model.

4. *Consolidating a Corporate Structure:* The corporate structure that offers the greatest promise for realizing the firm's financial objectives is identified. The firm can select its structure from any arrangements of organization components and their interrelationships.

5. *Formulating Corporate Policy:* Corporate policy directs what considerations are to be given weight in operational decisions. The meaning of the term "policy" and the uses to which it is put may vary widely, depending on who is using it and in what context. It is employed here to identify tenets of the corporation—the attitudes, assumptions, beliefs, and values that constitute the background of decision and action. Policy is fundamental. It represents the intellectual and operational foundations on which the company's business decisions are built.

6. *Specifying Principles Governing Development Require-*

ments: Deliberate development is essential to a corporation's survival, profitability, and growth. "Development" includes product, process, and market development but is not limited to these. It encompasses human resources and management development and organization development, including the continuous correction of outmoded business and behavioral elements in the firm's culture.

When completed, the Ideal Strategic Corporate Model should define and specify all these elements for the company. However, the major elements are not considered separately and independently. One is discussed after another to a point of tentative agreement and final specifications are reached only after each part has been interrelated with all others to provide a cohesive and congruent whole.

The Power of Models

A completed design for an Ideal Strategic Corporate Model provides a corporation with objectives. It gives a framework within which sound tactical and operational decisions can be made. It can focus and concentrate the thinking, motivations, and energies of corporate excellence. A corporate model of excellence can offer another positive effect: When an ideal model of what is possible is contrasted with the existing situation, a gap is created and significant motivational energy is released to close it. When Phases 1 through 3 have been completed, corporate members eagerly await key leadership decisions to acquire excellence. They are prepared to commit their efforts to moving away from the current situation. Their energies not only can be released, but they also can be dedicated to corporate objectives. The conditions under which personal gratification can be attained from corporate contribution are widely present. Not only are key executives ready and capable of exercising leadership, but the base of the organization is more fully ready to receive it.

Understanding of what an Ideal Strategic Corporate Model is, and what it is not, is essential for seeing the manner in which it can influence the strengthening of a corporation. An Ideal Strategic Corporate Model is *not:*

1. A projection of the future based on what has been accomplished in the past.

2. A mechanical adding up of the status quo segments of the company plus a "hip pocket" or emotionally charged 10 or 15 percent improvement factor.

3. A "cloud nine," twenty-first-century model of a bright new world.

4. A generalized statement of the corporate virtues that persons should aspire to achieve.

5. An obliteration of the past by rejecting all of what tradition, precedent, and past practice constitute.

An Ideal Strategic Corporate Model *is:*

1. A vision of the future formulated without adhering to dictates of the past.

2. The use of sound business logic to develop guidelines for corporate direction in six key areas: Key Financial Objectives, Nature of the Business, Nature of the Market, Corporate Structure, Corporate Policy, and Development Requirements.

3. A blueprint for action that enables a corporation to design specific and concrete tactics of implementation.

4. Systematic thinking that promotes creative and innovative solutions to problems that had come to be tolerated and accepted.

5. The identification of opportunities previously recognized or discounted as not worth the effort.

Executive Level Designing

The people involved in Phase 4 are those with ultimate responsibility for the direction and character of the corporation's future. Implementation activities, which include detailed tactical planning to change from the existing operation to the ideal, are carried out later by designated individuals or task forces. In the case of the latter, membership is drawn from the top and from echelons beneath it. For example, part of the Phase 4 model might be an acquisition strategy. This may involve the vice president in charge of corporate development or long-range planning at some point in the implementation process. Key members of executive management, therefore, engage in the study, deliberation, and decision making in this phase of Grid OD.

The chief executive officer and other members of executive management accountable for the conduct of the firm are active participants if the development unit is the corporation. If the Grid OD unit is a subordinate component such as a plant, those who engage in the design of an Ideal Strategic Corporate Model should include at least the corporate vice president of manufacturing, the plant manager, and key managers who report to that person. If the unit is a marketing region, those who engage in this activity include the vice president of marketing, the regional marketing manager, and his or her key executive group, and so on.

This means that Phase 4 designing, which anticipates where the company will be in the next five, ten, fifteen or more years, cannot be delegated. The top executive and top team are responsible for the corporation's strategy since they have the widest overall perspective. They have the responsibility for leading the corporation, ultimate control over the resources—financial, material, and personnel—which must be committed if any goals are to be achieved. Thus the top team is the natural unit for constructing the Ideal Strategic Corporate Model. Participation by the top team is only a first approximation, however. Upon further examination, it may or may not be found to be the actual team for designing the model.

Almost without exception, the top executive participates as a member of the team that constructs the model. Other members of the top team ordinarily complete the membership. There may, however, be members of the top team whose contribution is so specific and specialized that they have neither the experience, knowledge, nor responsibility to contribute the kind of thinking that is required. By the same token, there *may* be other members of the organization who are not members of the top team but whose experience, knowledge, and responsibilities are such that their participation in the design can make an essential contribution.

Selection for membership of the designing team for the Ideal Strategic Corporate Model is deliberate rather than taken for granted. The following criteria apply:

- Are all key decision makers who need to understand and to be committed to the design to ensure its effective implementation included?

- Are there members of the top team whose responsibilities are so narrow and specialized that their participation in the design or involvement in its implementation is wasteful?

- Are there other members of the firm who by virtue of experience, knowledge, or responsibility can be expected to make a significant contribution to the design or its implementation and who should therefore be included?

Strategy of Study and Design

Completing the design of an Ideal Strategic Corporate Model may or may not take an extended period of time. The point is to take as much time as necessary to bring it to a successful conclusion. To provide some approximation of time, we can say that a month is short, whereas a year is long. Most companies fall somewhere in between. And, all the while, business as usual is taking place and organizational matters are receiving the requisite attention.

The initial formulation involves a period of concentrated effort when key managers free themselves from day-to-day corporate activities. Designing the model is accomplished through an instrumented approach including prestudy materials, a background text, and structured Phase 4 tasks. It employs a variety of learning strategies to facilitate the investigation essential for constructing such a model. The instruments used provide a general approach and a point of departure. As with other phases, a Grid OD Senior Consultant assists. This individual makes a contribution by supporting the effort rather than directing it. The OD consultant may be brought in from the outside, or an internal consultant may have been trained to take this role.

The first step requires executives to develop convictions about the key elements of business logic fundamental to the operation of any corporation. Executives complete their individual study and then discuss and agree on the elements of the ideal corporate strategy. The objective of the background preparation is to give those responsible for designing the model access to the same concepts of business logic.

Study of the corporation as it currently is run is the next subject of examination. Against the framework of agreed-on precepts of sound business logic, actual practices can be viewed with greater objectivity. Having identified discrepancies between sound logic and current operations, executive management designs an Ideal Strategic Corporate Model. Much progress in completing the design of such a model is possible within the period of several days of concentrated effort. Further examination of specific corporate objectives, practices, or problems over weeks or months may be required, however, before fundamental agreements can become final and binding.

The completed Ideal Strategic Corporate Model is a necessary foundation for reforming or strengthening a company. Yet, without clear ways by which it can be brought into actuality, it is little more than an abstraction. The final activity during the Phase 4 week, therefore, investigates ways to get the model implemented. It leads to an outline of the steps for putting the model into actual operation in Phase 5, which starts with the first steps of implementation.

Lower Level Critique and Recommendation

Once completed by the top team, the Ideal Strategic Corporate Model is distributed for review, evaluation, and critique; for testing of implications; and for stimulating recommendations for strengthening it. The number of layers of the corporation involved in this step cannot be specified in advance, but there are two specific objectives in who should review the model. One is to ensure that the best thinking within the corporation has contributed to the final model. The other is to develop widespread understanding of it. The contribution of lower levels can be through their recommendations. The decision step, which may or may not be congruent with these recommendations, is a top-level responsibility that in the final analysis cannot be taken by anyone but the chief executive.

The significance of lower level critique in the Phase 4 activity cannot be overemphasized. Seldom do those below see strategic corporate plans except in their final form. Prior participation is rarely sought except from those directly involved and responsible for ultimate decision making. However, by seeking critique and recommendations from lower level groups, not only is it possible to tighten up the model, but it also becomes feasible to solicit creative and innovative additions as well and to identify aspects that may be impractical. It constitutes "reality testing." Equally important is the buy-in that arises when people have the opportunity to examine, evaluate, and think through a plan of action before it takes the form of a directive.

Timing

If designing an Ideal Strategic Corporate Model is at the core of corporate effectiveness, why is it not done as the first Grid OD activity? The rationale for the sequence of Phase 1 to 2 to 4 is that it provides perspective. In a few experimental Grid OD projects, the design of an Ideal Strategic Corporate Model was the first activity undertaken. In no case was the experiment a success. The best explanation for the lack of results from starting Grid OD with the Ideal Strategic Corporate Model is that communication blockages within the executive level of management prevented effective and committed effort from taking place. Management had not eliminated barriers to communication, which included win/lose power struggles, the unwitting readiness to compromise and accommodate, and unthinking acceptance of traditions, precedents, and past practices. The designs that were produced were so lacking in substance that they failed to provide a sound foundation for moving the corporation toward excellence. Furthermore, operational levels of management were not prepared to act with the energy and dedication needed to move the model from the drawing board to implementation. Solving communication problems before designing an Ideal Strategic Corporate Model seems to represent the soundest order of events while running minimum risk of failure.

Beyond the fact that Phase 2 at the top needs to be completed before the Ideal Strategic Corporate Model is begun, another matter of timing should be considered. If the organization is engulfed in dealing with an urgent and pervasive organization difficulty or crisis, it is probably better to resolve that problem before engaging in Phase 4 design work. For example, if a strike were imminent or underway, or an oil spill is absorbing key executive attention, or a Bhopal has occurred, or a hurricane is moving in from the Caribbean, or whatever the case may be, it is unlikely that participants can sufficiently free themselves from such entanglements to engage in the demanding and complex thinking required to analyze an Ideal Strategic Corporate Model in an effective way. It is preferable to defer the design of the model until such distracting situations can be resolved.

Case Study: Launching a New Business Era

The company president and CEO initiated the task of designing an Ideal Strategic Corporate Model. The group to whom he was speaking was the top executive committee of a company doing $800 million in annual sales. The president had been in office ten years. He is one of the outstanding business leaders in a city of close to three million persons. The company is a long-established business firm and is a highly respected corporate citizen. It has four competitors. They are tough. The market is tough. The company objective of increasing market share has been realized each year over the past decade. The year-to-year gains, though modest, have been acceptable. Profits, however, have not shown a corresponding increase. It has been next to impossible to break through a stabilized plateau of earnings.

Grid Organization Development had been underway for a year and a half. Phases 1, 2, and 3 had been completed throughout the corporation. Development efforts had only increased the sense of uneasiness in the top team about the leadership and direction it had been giving to the company. They shared an acute awareness that fundamental change was needed to achieve corporate excellence. Throughout the company there was a sense of anticipation that the executive group would set a new course that would move the organization off its plateau to higher earnings ground.

"Our organization development work during the previous year and a half has been preparing us mentally and emotionally for a major shift in the whole concept of the business. If it is to be of any value, it will have to take an in-depth approach. We have to ask ourselves if we are ready to tackle this challenge in a fundamental and objective manner. Are we prepared to throw the company book out of the window and look at our investments from a fresh point of view?"

In response to this challenge, the top team committed to undertake a Phase 4 effort.

Challenging the Status Quo

"When you score our past years against the hard yardstick of business reality, none of us has been satisfied to supervise the ineffective effort that we have turned in," the president said. "I am as dissatisfied as you are. You work hard and I work hard, but we have failed to produce a result that we can be proud of or gratified by in the future. This is not because of lack of effort or commitment but due to the definition of the business as it now stands.

"I don't believe we are prepared to continue in the present form. We must change the nature and scope of the business. We must create a new model that has a radically different objective. As I see it, based on the capital we have available, the objective of our business is to make the optimum rate of return on assets and maintain it for a long time. Our only purpose is to increase our profitability. We want to expand our market share but only under the condition that we are able to do so through earning a good return on assets employed."

The eight-person top team, whose membership included the chairman, the president and CEO, and vice presidents in charge of international operations, administration, manufacturing and engineering, marketing, human resources, and corporate planning, was on the threshold of designing an ideal strategic model. A discussion in the boardroom of two of the six key elements—establishing the financial objectives and designing the corporate structure—is presented to reflect the quality and character of thinking in this effort. The deliberations that went into the complete model ranged far beyond what is reported here. Brief summaries of portions of the discussion of these two key elements, however, show the character of thinking as well as the history of past traditions and attitudes that suggest why a profit plateau had been reached.

Clarifying Financial Objectives

Historically, financial objectives expressed in numerical terms had not been used as sharp, crisp guidelines of business thought. In the company, the conventional approach was to preset budgets on a yearly basis with a quarterly review of deviations from the budget as a control device. The stated concern was to "get volume up," to gain a larger share of market. Percent of market had always been an important target. Organization members were comfortable when it was increasing. They were "up" when market share was up, "down" when market share was on the decline. Although profit was somewhere in the background, they felt impelled to get percent of market even higher.

The implicit faith was that with a preset budget and increased sales volume, profit would go up. When indications of a softening market appeared, additional funds were poured into advertising and promotion. As the top tried to develop explicit financial objectives, as shown in Table 9-1, they recognized the mental barriers of their deeply entrenched thinking.

There were two causes of the shift in thinking from a market share orientation to a return on investment concept. One was the heightened objectivity made possible by the top team's viewing the corporation from the eyes of stockholders. The argument was that in the final analysis, increases in earnings per share and a sustained improvement of the price of the stock are the ultimate tests that stockholders apply when making an investment decision. The soundness of this business logic is indisputable. Moreover, one manager pointed out that a significant number of employees were share owners. For this reason, it was maintained that these new financial objectives would be widely supported throughout the corporation.

The second argument that proved convincing was related to difficulties encountered in debt financing in the past. The management team knew that the banking community was not impressed by their financial performance and was therefore reluctant to lend money for further capital investment. If the company were to take full advantage of growth opportunities, there was no alternative except to manage the corporation in such a way as to increase banker confidence. Both of these considerations compelled members of this top team to adopt the position that they must shift their thinking and center their action on improving return on investment. This in turn led to the conviction that the corporation should be reorganized in ways that would permit and assist all managers to apply the same kind of financial thinking to their business decisions.

The next task was to set a minimum return on investment. The concern here was that if the minimum were to be set higher than current levels of performance, managers failing

Table 9–1
*Genuine Concern with the Organization's Earning Capacity
Results from Designing an Ideal Strategic Corporate Model*

From	To
Maintain or increase market share while living within a budget.	Optimal 30, minimum 20 percent pretax return on assets employed with an unlimited time horizon.
Dollar profit should improve and not fall behind last year. Return on investment computed and discussed on an after-the-fact calculation that exerted little or no influence on operational decision making.	Each business unit should have a specified profit improvement factor to be calculated on a business-by-business basis. The objective should be an earnings per share level that would within five years justify a price-earnings ratio of 17 to 1 or better.
	Share of market objectives should be established within the framework of return on assets and cash generation objectives.

to meet it would think it unfair and arbitrary. There was also a fear that an across-the-board minimum would not reflect realities of various segments and that this top-management–imposed standard would result in defeatism. On the other hand, if the minimum were to be set too low, those businesses operating above it would tend to feel complacent and satisfied and would have little incentive to strive for higher profitability. It also was agreed that they might be inclined to raise the minimum at a later time. This, they were convinced, would be resisted and reacted to adversely by the rest of the management group. Despite these difficulties, they were able to face and deal with the challenge of committing the organization to the highest possible financial objectives.

Many alternatives were considered when the values shown in Table 9–1 were finally set. The top team analyzed the return on investment and rate of growth of the top 5 percent of the forty companies in the same broad industrial category as their own. "If other managements operating under similar conditions of product and market can accomplish these results," they reasoned, "why can't we?" This argument had overwhelming force, for it emphasized a key factor of actual difference in financial performance: managerial competence and high standards of striving.

Many opinions were voiced on the special circumstances in the company that would make these standards unfair. One by one these reservations were examined, often with the result that the team found that although many differences *did* exist, they could be eliminated by a determined management. The arguments that occurred and the conflicts they produced could be dealt with successfully because they had already developed strong convictions about 9,9 management and faced and resolved many communication barriers in their own Team Building activity in Phase 2. The rest of the firm, furthermore, had demonstrated in Phases 1 through 3 that there was an undercurrent of eagerness for a strong indication of new direction. The objectivity achieved resulted in their rejecting the convenient rationalization that "our company is different." It permitted members to acknowledge openly organization indulgences, overstaffing, unneeded headquarters services, and many examples where profit improvement could be realized if there was a strong will to achieve better results.

Changing the Corporate Structure

Headquarters' structure was the result of evolutionary changes rather than a deliberate plan for effective integration of people into the organization's objectives. Over the years, managers had been asked to expand services, which had resulted in a top-heavy headquarters staff. In addition, executive dining rooms, car and chauffeur services, and a variety of other perquisites were identified. They were difficult to justify. Furthermore, though the headquarters people were hard working, they were applying attention to many nonessential activities or were overly concerned with detail. Manufacturing and marketing management in the headquarters group had been devoting a great deal of time to the most minute aspects of operational budgets and expenses. Hiring, firing, salary, pricing, market promotions—all required approval. Even a modification in a small volume product or a minor manufacturing technological innovation rallied them to protracted discussion in the boardroom. Daily dealing with the most minor matters had become a way of life.

As the top team designed an ideal corporate structure, current arrangements thwarted them at every turn. As their thoughts crystallized, they became convinced, sometimes painfully so, of the severity of actions that would be required if the company were to be turned around. Table 9–2 shows this shift. Spurred on to think through an ideal model, they agreed that the company should be decentralized by product line, with each product line established to permit the determination of its profit contribution as a percentage of the assets required to support it.

By structuring planning, marketing, manufacturing, product development, and support service functions in integrated components, and providing measurements geared to financial objectives, managers would be able to make the same kinds of judgments in their business decisions as are made by investors in choosing between two companies. Managers would have the authority and responsibility essential for the decisions that affect rate of return on investment. Several results were expected. First, they would have control over operational, personnel, and financial matters that directly and indirectly affect rate of return. They then would in effect be operating their own businesses. Reinforced by minimum and optimal rates of return on investment, motivation to organization excellence would reach its maximum height. Performance appraisal as a part of salary review and extra compensation determination would be directly correlated to measured contributions. Finally, the basis of measurement is something to which people could and would commit themselves fully because the corporate business logic would square with personal business logic. Headquarters' control would be through selecting strong, effective managers, approving budget and capital appropriations, and setting clear policy.

Table 9–2
Need for Organization Structure Changes Becomes Obvious as a
Result of Designing an Ideal Strategic Corporate Model

From	To
Heavy headquarters staff with regulatory and procedural control over each of nine geographical regions.	A decentralized product-line organization with management and control geared to key financial objectives, with the local option to purchase from other autonomous units or on the open market. Marketing and manufacturing responsibility decentralized. Headquarters' control maintained through the approval of the capital budget and setting of policy. Minimum headquarters staff.

The final formulation of what the organization structure should be did not come easily. Members unwittingly introduced unexamined assumptions into the planning discussions. This proved to be the biggest barrier. To minimize this effect, the top team listed each assumption, keeping the list before them as the various alternatives about how the business might be arranged were developed. Only in this way were they able to deal with the pressures of history and tradition.

A few members felt that they could not establish an equitable basis for appraising plant, equipment, and property across a wide range of different circumstances. Old plant and equipment on expensive downtown property, new and automated equipment in modern plants on industrial park property, property in some cases benefited by favorable tax considerations, represented some of the variables. Other members maintained that ground rules could be established that would provide a basis for just and equitable comparison across these variables for an extended period of time. Their argument was that this kind of financial engineering was difficult to accomplish and necessarily must be in a series of steps, moving from coarse to refined. The concept they decided to pursue was replacement value of plant and equipment, which eliminated most of the variables that were historical and immutable. Resistance to structuring in this manner crumbled when one executive who had had managerial experience in another company was able to describe in rich detail the way this had been accomplished and the constructive consequences that had resulted for more effective management. The conclusion was, "Since we know it has been done, the reason for reluctance must be that we don't want to face up to the comfortable rationalizations that keep us from taking action based on financial judgments. If others can do it, there's no reason why we can't. The problem is attitude and motivation."

Another question that wrenched at tradition was, "Are the many services grafted onto headquarters really essential to effective operations, or are they there only because we've become accustomed to them?" This arose when it was clear that segmented businesses were desirable as the basis for organization structure.

"How could business segments obtain genuinely essential services? Does it necessarily follow that those services are always best provided by headquarters?" The initial reaction was "Yes," because it had always been done that way. As this question was discussed, the conclusion reached was that headquarters, under a product-line, return-on-investment concept of structure, should only provide:

1. Those services that three or more business product segments requested and were willing to pay for as an expense under their key financial objectives; or

2. Those services that were deemed essential for intelligent headquarters supervision and carried out as a headquarters expense.

This formulation was backed by the conviction, now firm, that genuine achievement motivation is the result when a business manager has control over his or her key costs and income decisions. Under this kind of formulation, it became evident that staff services retained would be streamlined and held at an essential minimum.

Another issue that had to be faced squarely if the new thinking were to be implemented was, "If a service or line of business is to be divested, this will involve far more than disposing of machines, desks, or cafeteria equipment. It means terminating long-service employees—some of whom have worked for this company thirty-five years."

Personnel disruption created in major reorganization is harsh, real, and inescapable. There is no easy path around this issue. The attitude and resolution developed by this top team was that they *could* anticipate the impact from these kinds of personnel disruptions. It *could* be minimized by retraining and reassignment to existing vacancies in other parts of the business; early retirement; retirement counseling; extended advance notice; making known to employees vacancies and opportunities in other companies within the area; reemployment counseling; and just severance pay.

They saw that if these issues were not faced, it would be to the long-term detriment of the profitability of the business and that of present and future employees. To ensure equitability to all concerned, the top team agreed that personnel reduction decisions caused by reorganization would be made according to criteria of competence rather than present job requirements or individual skills. If the skills of those affected were not appropriate to the new organization structure, they would be offered reassignment. This would be done, where practical, by providing on-the-job development assignments and retraining. Thus separations resulting from reorganization would affect those least competent.

Finalizing the Ideal Strategic Corporate Model

After completing the discussion on the other four elements, top management presented the ideal model to the next level of management for study, testing, evaluation, criticism, and recommendations for modification, revisions, extensions, and deletions. Lower levels of management were thus provided a full opportunity to contribute to matters of vital significance to them. Points of difference generating conflict were identified. In a sequence of discussions that extended over a period of several months, these points of difference were effectively resolved, some by executive management's shifting a previously held point of view and some by shifting at lower levels. Some of the issues of disagreement found effective resolution through the exploration and identification of new formulations that had not appeared in the model and that had been formulated by lower levels. The significant aspect of this step was that understanding and agreement based on insight into the strategy and its implications provided the basis for the ideal model as it took operational shape.

Once the top team and the level of management immediately beneath them had discussed and agreed on the model, it became the subject of a team action seminar throughout the corporation, with managers at all levels studying, discussing, and evaluating its subtleties and implications. This was done with the understanding that if parts of the model were found unsound, they could still be modified and changed. Thus the entire management organization was offered an opportunity to challenge the ideal model and, on the basis of their own testing of its logic, to convince themselves of its soundness. The company now has an understood and agreed-on strategy to guide its long-term development.

Implementing the Model: Phase 5

Phase 5 is the implementation stage of the Ideal Strategic Corporate Model. The idea is not to tear down the whole company and start from scratch but rather to remodel the firm according to the blueprint developed in Phase 4. Phase 5 identifies and implements the action steps necessary for shifting the company from "old" to "new."

Having completed the Phase 4 model, there are two forward paths the top team can take. The choice is between a gradual implementation of the Phase 4 design or a more vigorous and systematic approach to implementation. The first represents gradual change, whereas the second characterizes a sustained Grid OD effort. We describe both, however, as this is a critical point in an organization's future growth and progress.

The Gradual Approach

Sometimes the urgency of business matters makes it difficult, if not impossible, to marshal the degree of energy necessary for bringing the model into quick and effective use. The decision often has been to go about the Phase 4 implementation in a more gradual way, one piece at a time, implementing a policy here or a policy there, or bringing about a limited organization restructuring, or shifting the nature of the market as "natural" opportunities arise to make this possible.

As problems arise, an attempt is made to reach solutions congruent with the Ideal Strategic Corporate Model. Such problems may have persisted for some time, and now they are subject to reevaluation as the opportunities present themselves. Decisions regarding barriers to change and new opportunities are weighed against the model as they appear. We see this as a gradual approach to change. The danger is that the organization will return to old ways of operating—tradition, precedent, and past practice—and the likelihood of lasting and enduring change is placed at risk.

The Systematic Approach

The systematic approach is quite different. Here the goal is deliberate and widespread intervention aimed at bringing the corporation in line with the blueprint developed in Phase 4. A series of steps provides the basis for accomplishing this.

The organization is first subdivided into components, a component being the smallest grouping of interrelated activities that produces a recognizable source of earnings and identifiable cost or expense. Another step is to compute the investment related to these activities tied up in facilities, equipment, and personnel. After these steps have been taken, it becomes possible to evaluate whether the business activity identified by that component meets or can be changed to meet the specifications of the model. The idea is that these organization subcomponents can pass the test of operating as profit centers or strategic business units.

For example, transfer prices for incoming materials and services may be set in line with what the same material or service might be procured at from external sources. Therefore, if the internal unit cannot be competitive with alternative sources of supply, it must be reformulated in such a way that it can achieve this objective. This may require combining two units to create a new and viable entity.

If the unit is unable to achieve this status, it becomes necessary to consider divestment with the organization contracting for the supplies or services at more favorable terms.

A number of questions can be asked to evaluate the viability of the units as restructured according to the Phase 4 model. Is this profit center currently realizing a return on investment consistent with the model? If not, are there controllable expenses or pricing factors that can be altered to bring it into line? Is this area of business activity consistent with market areas identified by the model as areas of sound and desirable growth? These questions are characteristic of the many employed to determine whether each segregated activity should be expanded, shortened, changed, or eliminated in pursuing corporate development.

When a systematic approach to Phase 5 implementation has taken place, decisions regarding mission, investment, divestment, organization structure, human resource development, and policies surrounding all of these areas can be considered and set in motion by the top team. As a result of this rigorous and thorough testing of organization viability, the decisions made and implementation steps that follow are based on the soundest thinking and informed judgment available, rather than the result of happenstance or armchair speculation. Phase 5 implementation can produce a quantum leap in organization productivity because of the depth of change involved.

Phase 6: Stabilization and Consolidation

Phase 6 constitutes an end of a sequence and, often, a new beginning. This activity is used to stabilize and consolidate the progress achieved in the preceding Phase 1–5 efforts before recycling into another period of change.

There are three key reasons why such a step is important. Managing change is the opposite of managing the tried and true. People tend to repeat the latter, but they are more likely to lose interest, commitment, or courage to continue with what is novel and unpredictable. Such reduced effort may lead to failure. A second reason to undertake Phase 6 is that continued study and analysis of progress made may assist in the identification of new opportunities and directions for organizational thrust. A third is that changes in the external environment may dictate the need for modifications in the course of action. The monitoring activities of Phase 6 provide a basis for doing so.

In summary, Phase 6 is a period of looking backward; a review and reflection on what has been accomplished and what remains to be done. It is a critique of the whole, as well as an assessment of each of its parts. It stimulates the concentration of effort on rectifying remaining weaknesses and tendencies to fall back into old ways. But, as new possibilities come in to view that previously could not have been seen, it also is a point of beginning. Sometimes it celebrates the passing of the baton from one leadership generation to the next; this is particularly so when a significant portion of the management that initiated the OD efforts has been replaced by new people who seek a challenge of their own creation and design. We will not elaborate further on these two stages as significant writing is available elsewhere regarding Phases 5 and 6 of Grid Organization Development.[1]

Summary

Precepts of business logic are no less in the history of a company than are the behavioral practices of its culture. Dealing with behavioral practice is an important step toward excellence but an incomplete one by itself. Taking the step that results in strengthening its business logic permits a company to fuse sound behavior with valid business practice. This is the hallmark of corporate excellence. In Phase 4, business traditions and rules of thumb are challenged by the most rigorous business logic. The aim is to examine the present business practices searchingly rather than taking them for granted.

Through this approach, corporate leaders can identify and evaluate the assumptions on which the corporation has been built and is operated. These assumptions are tested for validity. Those that are unacceptable are rejected and replaced with others that are sound. In this way, executive leadership can study the corporation, free itself from past and present thinking, and gear the organization up for strongest possible business action.

When the difficult decision to strive for a higher level of corporate excellence has been reached, all elements of business practice are subject to deliberate, detailed scrutiny. Only when existing assumptions have been tested and their soundness demonstrated is it valid to assume that limitations in thinking will have been identified and brought to an irreducible minimum. In this way, a corporation that is motivated to do so can achieve the conditions to excel.

Reference

1. Blake, R. R., and J. S. Mouton. 1968. *Corporate Excellence Through Grid Organization Development.* Houston: Gulf Publishing, pp. 241–272; and Blake, R. R. and J. S. Mouton. 1972. *How to Assess the Strengths and Weaknesses of a Business Enterprise.* Austin: Scientific Methods, Inc.

10

Grid OD in Perspective

Grid OD is a fundamental approach to change. Although it is no easy task to grasp its depth and implications, launching such an effort can prove invaluable for any organization. It may, in fact, determine corporate survival in the coming years. Neither evolution nor revolution is an attractive alternative to the deliberate exercise of intelligence in designing the future and in mobilizing human resources for achieving organization purpose.

Recognizing the importance of events in their true perspective calls for reality testing and objectivity. Doubt can result in missed opportunities, but it can also lead to increased thoroughness in inquiry, which in turn leads to greater objectivity. On the other hand, unharnessed enthusiasm can lead to actions not grounded in facts, but optimism supported by in-depth understanding of superordinate goals and objectives can nurture opportunities that otherwise might never come to fruition.

A recent example from the airline industry illustrates the powerful impact of a Grid Organization Development effort when implemented in an organization. The flight of UAL 811,[1] which suffered a structural failure when its cargo bay door blew open mid-flight, illustrates the concept of sound teamwork. Flying out of Honolulu en route to New Zealand and Australia, the plane, after suffering critical damage, was able to make a safe return to Hawaii. This was more than a fortuitous circumstance. The captain credited the crew's competence in mobilizing the necessary resources to solve the unique problems created by the hole in the fusilage as such damage relates to issues of decompression, which affect a safe descent.

According to the captain, in the past, crew members would have said nothing until after the crisis was over, instead making themselves available only to carry out the captain's commands. In this case, however, following Grid training and participating in annual refresher training, the crew was able to deliberate on the soundest course of action. This was critical in that consultation between the captain and first officer resulted in a sound decision being made on whether or not to lower the landing gear, as was standard procedure but which would have resulted in a high risk of crashing into the ocean. In a second instance, as they approached Honolulu, it was discovered that the wing flaps had been damaged on one side of the plane. Here essential information was provided by the first officer, resulting in a decision that led to a safe landing. In a third situation, the captain said that vital assistance was given by the second officer (flight engineer) regarding optimal landing speed based on the impaired condition of the aircraft.

All of this speaks for itself in terms of the magnitude of effective utilization of resources brought to bear upon the problem.

Grid OD penetrates to the core of a corporation's culture. Some of the changes such as those involving the behavioral social structure may take time to materialize, whereas others may be achieved immediately or realized along the way. To assess the full impact of Grid OD requires a long-term perspective in tracing cause and effect.

Barriers to Further Application

The commonsense assumption is that we can slide new knowledge into an old situation and in some way or other it will be used, that is, what *is* being done will stop and what *should be* done will replace it. It seems so logical to think that people will apply new concepts that make sense to them that rarely does anyone ask what the problems of application may actually be. This repeats the ten o'clock/two o'clock dilemma introduced in Chapter 1.

When a person starts trying to implement new concepts, often little or nothing happens because old ways have to be rejected before new ways can be accepted. Before this can happen, the old ways must be studied to determine why they are less acceptable than the new ways that can and should replace them. We must study the status quo to understand its inadequacies just as we study new options before accepting them as valid. This study and comparison of the old and new is the key to change.

How to Build a Dynamic Corporation

To transform the old culture, it is necessary to study and analyze it. The scope and depth of daily activities and actions in any company, however, rest on a silent organization. It is therefore difficult for people to see its underlying themes and patterns. Action cannot be stopped, frozen, or put in slow motion. As a result, the underlying patterns may remain obscure. Patterns of interactions and the values, attitudes, assumptions, and beliefs that people live by on a normative basis have evolved from traditions, precedents, and past practices. At any time they may become so uniformly accepted that they acquire a "second-nature" quality. Grid learning is therefore significant for continual, day-by-day design, analysis, and correction of the weaknesses and faults in these interaction patterns.

It is also important that everyone affected by the change engage in this study. Otherwise, managers are not prepared to embrace new approaches. Rather, they will continue to embrace the status quo. As a rule, people do not accept new ways on the basis of faith but rather defend old approaches on the basis of conventional wisdom. Therefore, all those affected by the change must participate in its application.

The Bigger Perspective

Our view is of the current status of American industry, which defines the circumstances to which Grid OD has been applied most frequently. In the conduct of business, the strategies of thinking and the techniques of analysis, measurement, control, and development presently employed are resulting in a significant underutilization of people and, therefore, of the financial and material resources that they manage. The degree of underutilization can only be guessed. Perhaps the average American company is achieving one-half of its potential. This is a significant underutilization of its human and, therefore, of its financial, material, and technical resources.

The results of tapping the wellsprings of human energies and making better use of concepts and techniques of business judgment and action can be great. The key to doing so is to be found in eliminating cultural drag, which promotes conformity and complacency, which blocks initiative and which stifles innovation. A strengthening of the human systems of individual behavior, team action, and intergroup relations enables managers to penetrate barriers to effectiveness on the business side of the firm. Through the design and implementation of an Ideal Strategic Corporate Model, it then becomes possible to generate the thrust so vital to the achievement and maintenance of corporate excellence.

A major human limitation to such action must be emphasized. It is the need for dealing with conflict in an open and confronting manner. When conflict is squarely faced, insight into differences is made possible. Alternative opinions can be examined that otherwise are not likely to emerge, and resolution based on maximum evidence, true commitment, and conviction is the result.

Furthermore, when conflict is faced, critique becomes an option. Critique is a key to the full utilization of human potential. It is a way of challenging the status quo by identifying sound alternatives that can produce stronger results than are currently being achieved. The ability to face disagreements that are inevitable when culture is challenged and to learn better ways by using critique is significant because it allows much of the currently untapped human potential to be mobilized in behalf of the corporation.

But there is another side to this coin. When people are engaged in this kind of common undertaking, when corporate-wide commitment to excellence is strong, they are living in a mature and adult manner, gaining the gratification from personal achievement that is possible only when their abilities are being fully employed. Mutual trust and respect come to replace unhealthy competitiveness, mutual recrimination, and win/lose power struggles.

The successful corporation is in a constant state of adaptation to both the external environment and to its own internal environment. Features of an organization operating in a sound manner include extensive two-way feedback and critique to assess effectiveness in achieving goals and standards of conduct with customers, suppliers, government entities, and so on. Critique of internal operations allows for constant reassessment of how well human, financial, and technical resources are being employed. This permits and stimulates determination of opportunities and challenges as well as risks and threats by all who are responsible for seizing opportunity and reducing risk.

Grid Organization Development is a systematic program through which a company can instill human motivations and emotions of involvement and commitment on an organization-wide basis. An almost limitless supply of human energy is available to be tapped when an organization is operating by standards of excellence. Energy is unleashed and funneled into finding creative and effective solutions to problems of production, quality, and sales, many of which may have plagued the company for years. In dynamic organizations that have attained this height of effectiveness, ordinary men and women are freed to act in extraordinary ways so that they come to know how to motivate and manage the problem-solving effort.

From this perspective, one of the last barriers to excellence—the human factor—can be integrated through participation, involvement, and commitment to valid corporate objectives as the organization and its members move into the future.

Reference

1. Valente, Judith, *The Wall Street Journal.* March 3, 1989, pp. C5, 3 Star Eastern Edition.